MADHUBANI ART

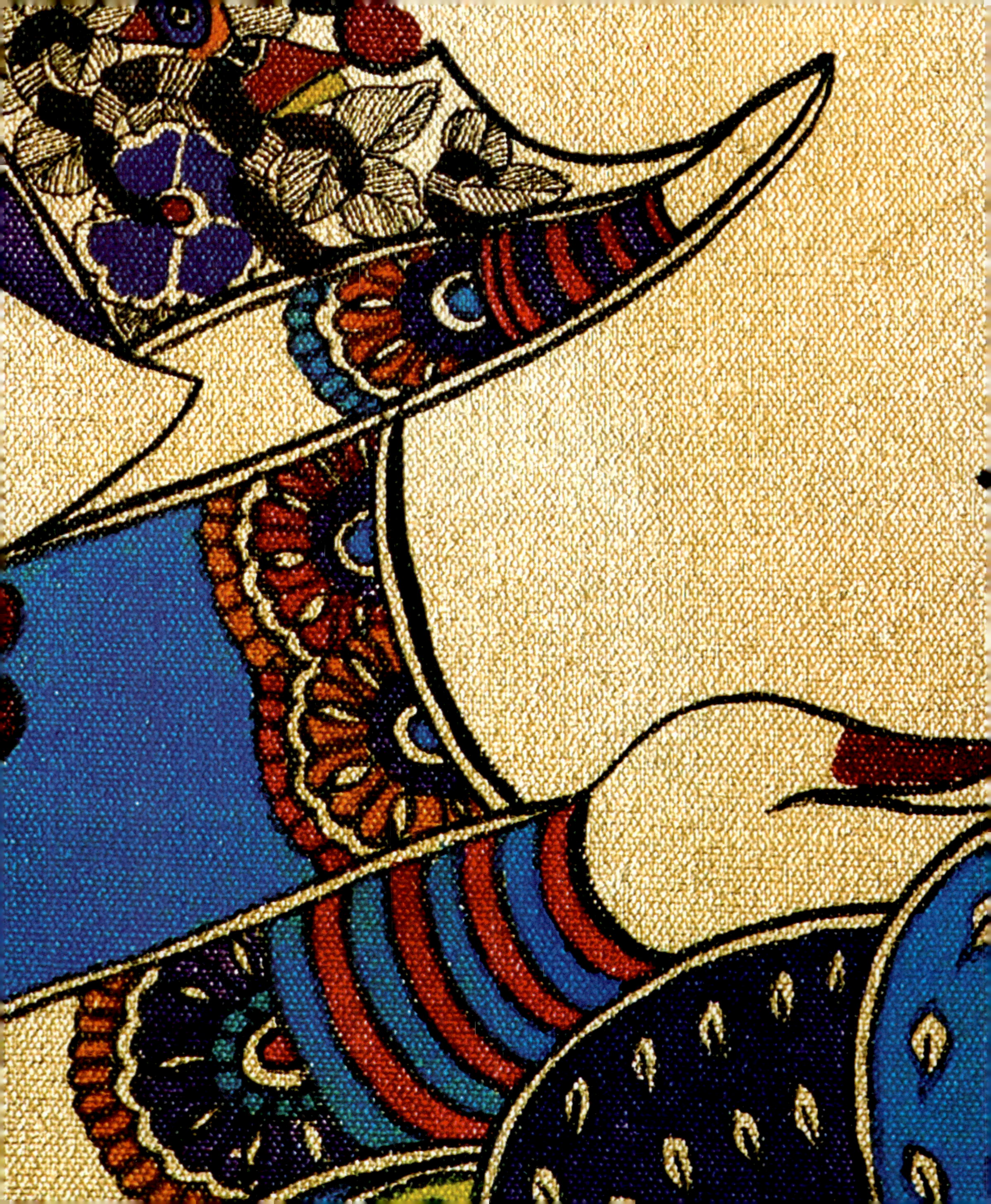

Indian Art Series

MADHUBANI ART

Bharti Dayal

MOSA
Museum of Sacred Art

NIYOGI BOOKS

Jointly published by

MOSA

MUSEUM OF SACRED ART

MOSA Belgium
Petite Somme 5,
6940 Septon,
Durbuy, Belgium
Tel: +32 (0) 86 43 30 22
Email: info@mosabelgium.com
Website: www.mosabelgium.com
http://www.radhadesh.com/

MOSA Italy
Via Scopeti 106/108,
San Casciano in Val di Pesa,
Florence, Italy – 50026
Tel: +39 (055) 820054
Email: info@mosaitaly.com
Website: www.mosaitaly.com
www.villavrindavana.net

NIYOGI BOOKS
D-78, Okhla Industrial Area, Phase-I
New Delhi-110 020, India
Tel: 91-11-26816301, 49327000
Fax: 91-11-26810483, 26813830
email: niyogibooks@gmail.com
website: www.niyogibooksindia.com

ISBN: 978-93-85285-08-0
Year of Publication: 2015
Reprint: 2024

Printed at: Niyogi Offset Pvt. Ltd., New Delhi, India

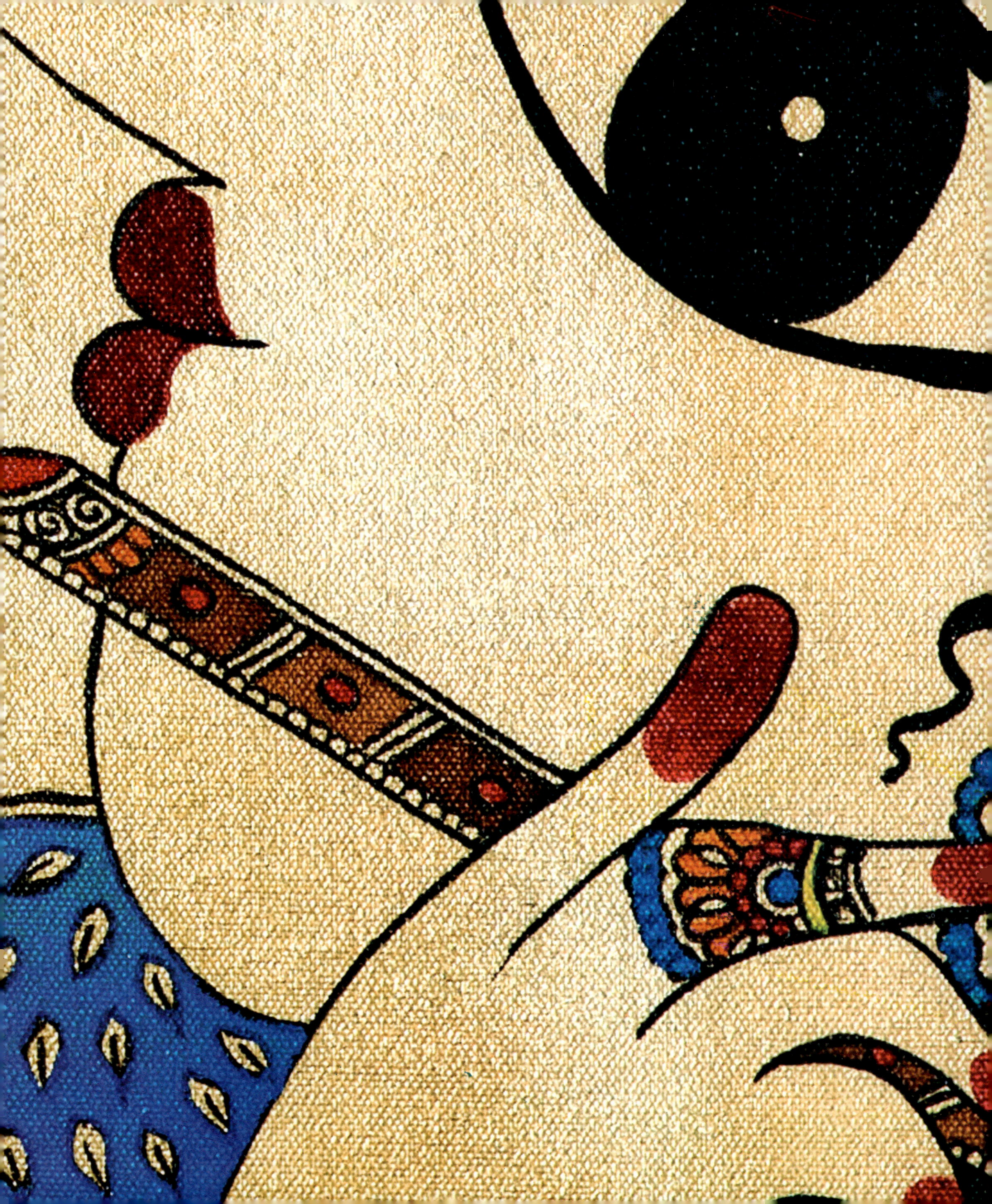

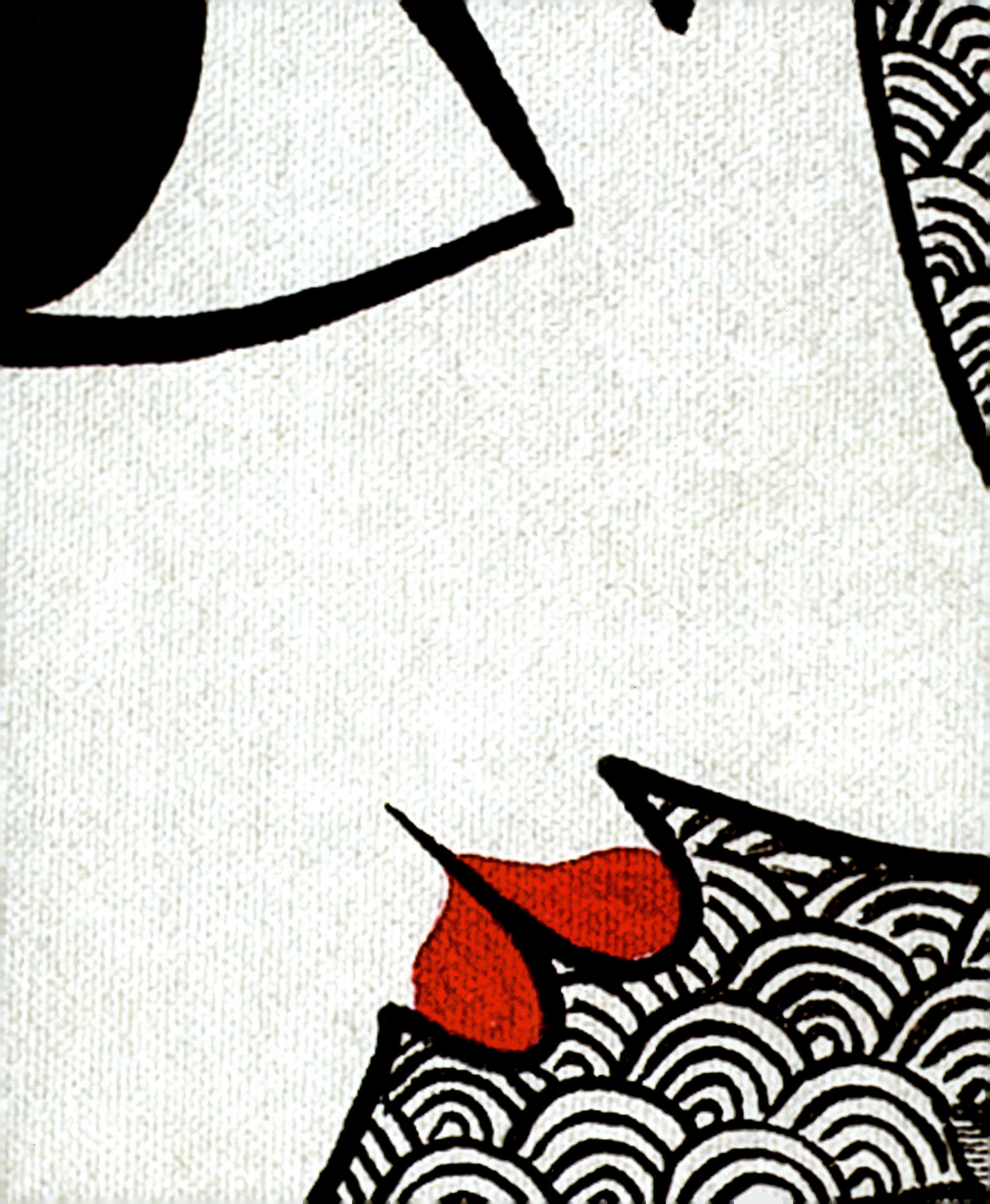

Contents

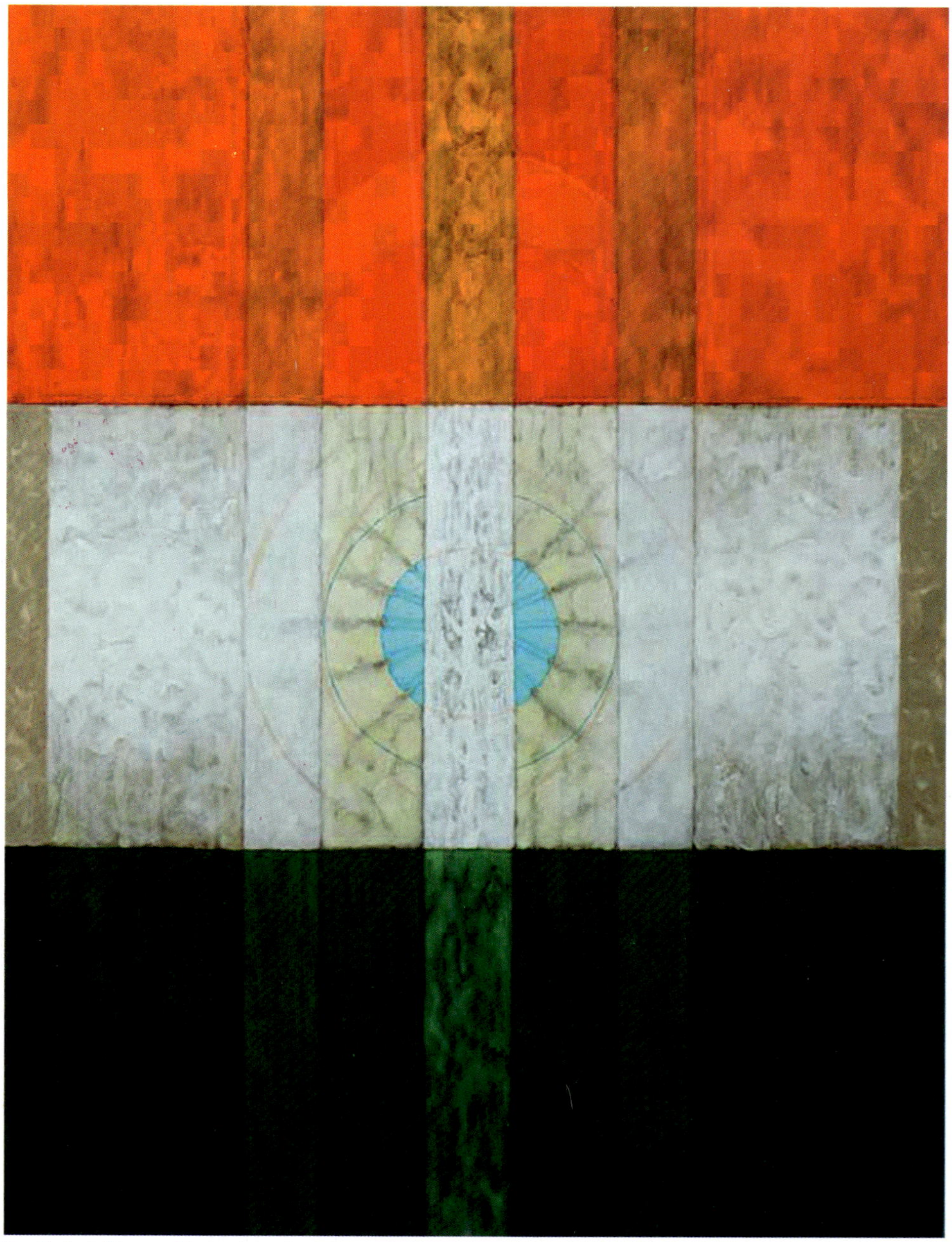

Om Prakash Sharma, Tiranga I, 2008

बेल्जियम, लक्ज़मबर्ग व यूरोपीय संघ में
भारत के राजदूत
Ambassador of India
to Belgium, Luxembourg and
the European Union

सत्यमेव जयते

Chaussee de Vleurgat 217
1050 Brussels, Belgium
Tel. : +32-2-645 1851
Fax : +32-2-640 9802
E-mail : ambassador@indembassy.be

"I am delighted that the prestigious Museum of Sacred Art of Belgium is organizing yet another exhibition relating to an Indian art form-- the renowned Madhubani Art from the Mithila region of Bihar in India.

Madhubani Art traces its origin to the great Indian epic "Ramayana" where it is believed that King Janaka of Mithila commissioned local artists to paint murals and decorate the town with this art form for the wedding of his daughter, Sita, to Lord Rama. Gradually, Madhubani art came to symbolise women's empowerment as women, in particular, began to paint pictures of gods and goddesses with an interpretation so divine that captured the hearts of many. Women have transmitted the beauty, love, care, environmental consciousness, traditions and faith incorporated in this art form for generations. Even today, villagers in the Mithila region of India decorate their homes and open spaces through colourful and vibrant depictions of mythological personalities of the great epics -- Ramayana and Mahabharata— in the Madhubani art form.

The elements of pattern and narrative of the Madhubani art form intertwine to present a beautiful artistic tradition that has survived the passage of time and has been brought to the modern times through the dedication and exceptional talents of artists like Ms. Bharti Dayal. I am glad that an Indian artist of the caliber of Ms. Bharti Dayal, the master of the Madhubani art form who has brilliantly adapted to depict it through the contemporary mediums of acrylic and canvas, is bringing her works for the art loving people of Belgium, in particular, and the west, in general.

The antiquity of Indian civilization matched by the vastness of its geographical extent has contributed to the rich and multiple art forms of India and I am glad that the Museum of Sacred Art has taken the commendable initiative to successfully present these art forms not only in Belgium, but also in the whole of Europe over the last six years since its inception. I deeply appreciate the initiative of the Museum to encourage interfaith dialogue through fine arts as manifested in its recent exhibitions—the "Forms of Devotion" held last year and the upcoming exhibition of Madhubani Art.

I am confident that the Indian art- loving people of Europe would once again have the opportunity to witness Indian mythology, icons and folk tales through the forthcoming exhibitions to relive the memories of the Europalia-India Festival last year.

I convey best wishes to the Museum of Sacred Art of Belgium for successful organization of the forthcoming exhibition that would be another tribute to the people of Belgium for their enthusiasm and love for Indian art".

M.S. Puri
Ambassador of India to Belgium, Luxembourg and the EU

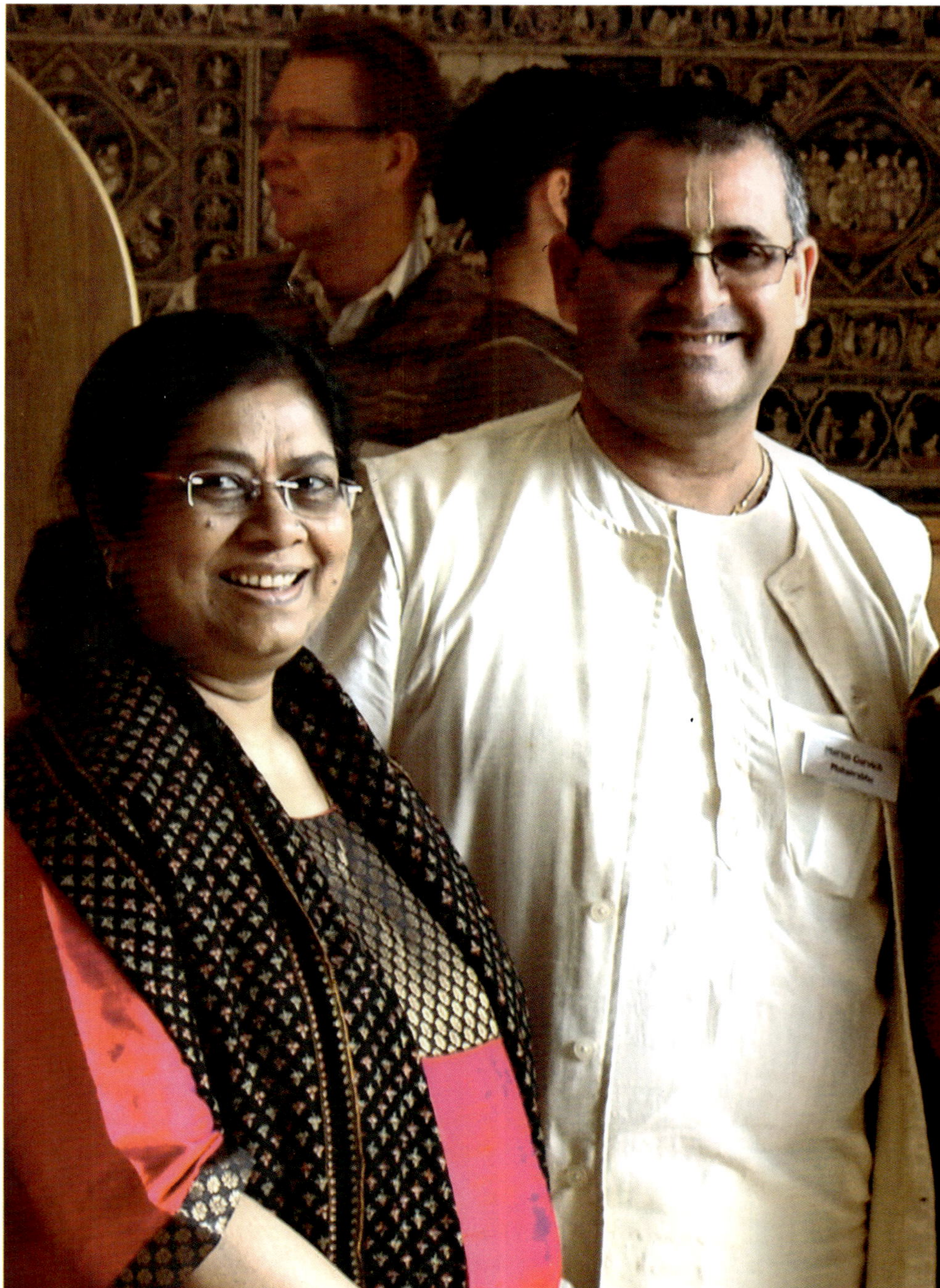

Bharti Dayal and Martin Gurvich (Director of MOSA)

Preface

It is with great pleasure that MOSA presents the show Madhubani Art, by Bharti Dayal. Bharti is one the first artists whose work we incorporated into MOSA's collection and the first with a sufficient number of works at MOSA to make a show. Dealing with her through the years has been inspiring, as she completely loves and identifies with this form of art. Her mastery of the tradition and her capacity to bring it out in contemporary media like acrylic and canvas have made her an ambassador to the modern world of this ancient art of Mithila. She is in love with both the tradition and its themes. The themes of Krishna, Radha and the gopis permeates her artwork. Her desire to put Krishna's unlimited pastimes on canvas keeps her devotion to Krishna alive and makes her very joyful. During this exhibition, Bharti will be giving live demonstrations and leading workshops on traditional Madhubani Art for MOSA's Western audiences, and we thank her for agreeing to do that. May the Western audiences enjoy the exuberant art of Bharti Dayal, full of colors, forms, patterns, and stories. This is the tradition of Madhubani Art that women have painted for millennia in the region of Mithila.

Martin Gurvich
Director of MOSA

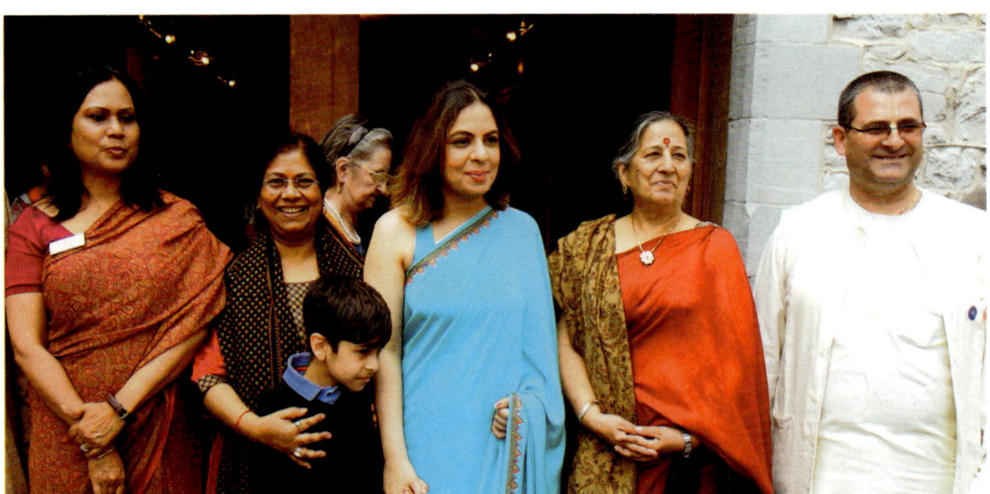

Imaging the Divine: Artscape of Bharti Dayal

Sushma K. Bahl

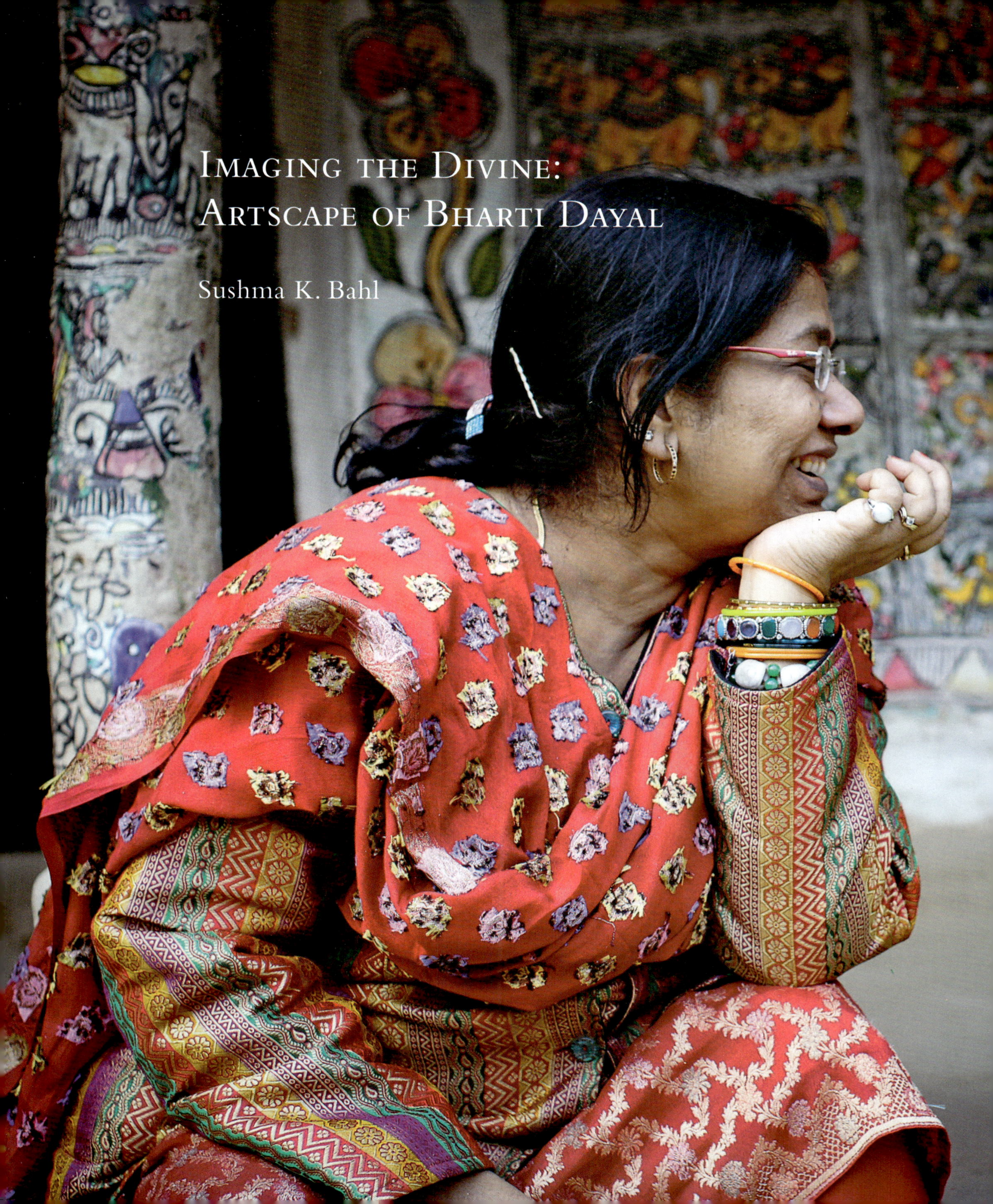

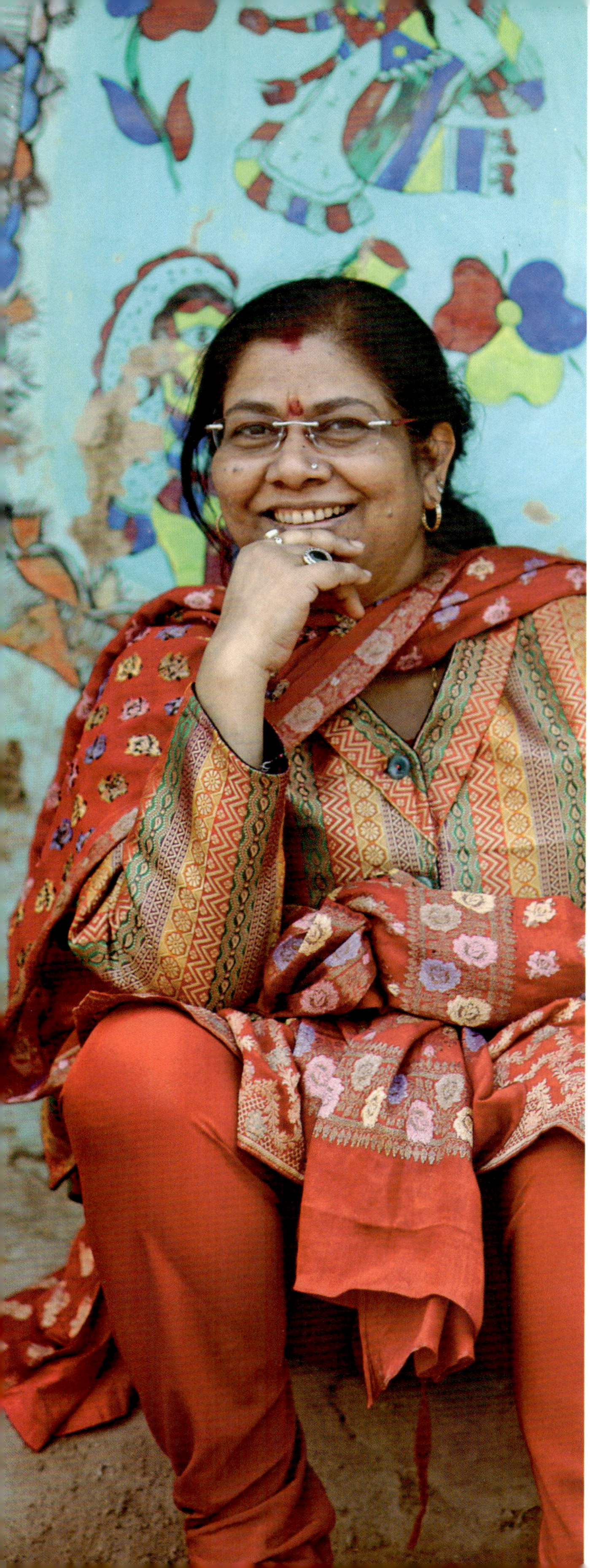

The art that Bharti Dayal practices, featuring divine forms and narratives amidst flora and fauna, can be literally described as *madhu* (honey) and *ban* (forest), i.e., a forest of honey, popularly known as Madhubani. The folk art form of the Mithila region of Bihar and parts of Nepal, the area located between the Himalayan foothills and the Gangetic plains, that goes back several eras, is perceived as *satyam*, *shivan* and *sundaram* (true, good and beautiful). With its distinct identity, themes, colouration and compositions, Madhubani art is a reflection of the reality and beauty of the life of the people of the Mithila region. And what artist Bharti Dayal does with her masterly strokes is expand the horizons of the form beyond the folk and craft domain into the wider gallery precincts in a more open and contemporary socio-cultural context.

Sushma K. Bahl (MBE), former head Arts & Culture (India) for the British Council, is an independent arts adviser, writer and curator of cultural projects including 'Forms of Devotion: The Spiritual in Indian Art'.

The Making of the Artist

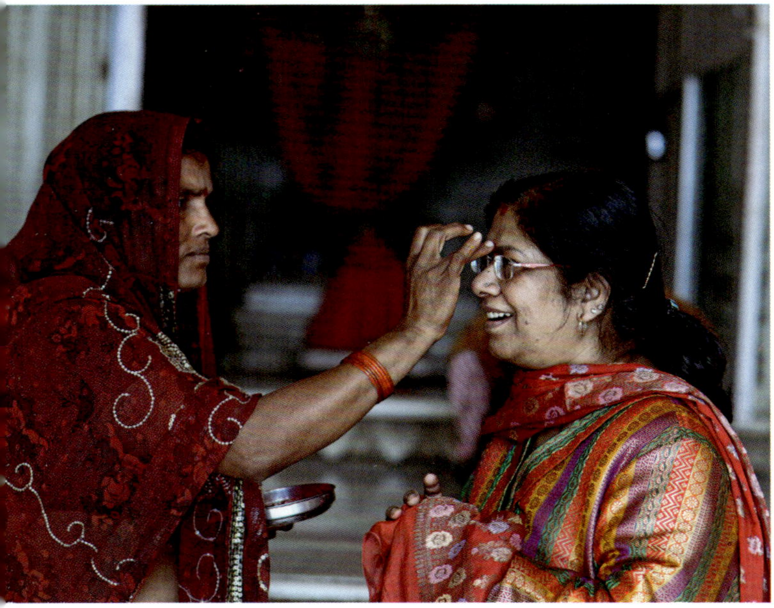

She was born at Samastipur in the Mithila region of Bihar. Painting came naturally to Bharti Dayal, who grew up in an ambience wherein art and aesthetics were part of everyday life. The eldest child, with four siblings, she spent a happy childhood in a close-knit joint family, with her uncles and aunts living within the vicinity. While her father worked in a government office, the other men folk worked on the family's agricultural land. The little girl helped her mother and aunts prepare the ground and learnt to paint on the floor and sketch epic scenes on the walls of the house, especially during festivals. She also learned embroidery and did appliqué work.

The village pond full of fish, the mango trees, the orchards and the temple in the vicinity were her playing fields on her way back from school. Given her passion for studies and a good academic track record, combined with the family's liberal views, she was sent to Darbhanga Mithila University, some distance away from home, where she stayed with her maternal grandmother for further studies. A hard-working and sharp student, she did well and passed BSc and MSc in Botany, both with gold medals. She also taught at Samastipur Womens College for a short period. In parallel with her academic interests she pursued her passion in art and continued to draw and paint regularly. Visiting the Kali Temple located on the university campus to pay her obeisance to the deity was on her daily agenda, as was painting.

"Art is in my blood," explains Bharti for whom painting is a passion and not a ritual. She pours her heart, mind and emotions into what she paints. "A smiling Radha can't be painted when one is angry." Her paintings are like writing, telling or enacting a story. As her work started attracting critical acclaim, she felt encouraged to shift her focus more towards the arts.

It was in 1986, after her marriage to Ajai, a chemical engineer, that she moved first to Jamshedpur, where he was working at that time (and in 1990 to Delhi). All through this period Bharti carried on with her painterly engagement, evolving and refining

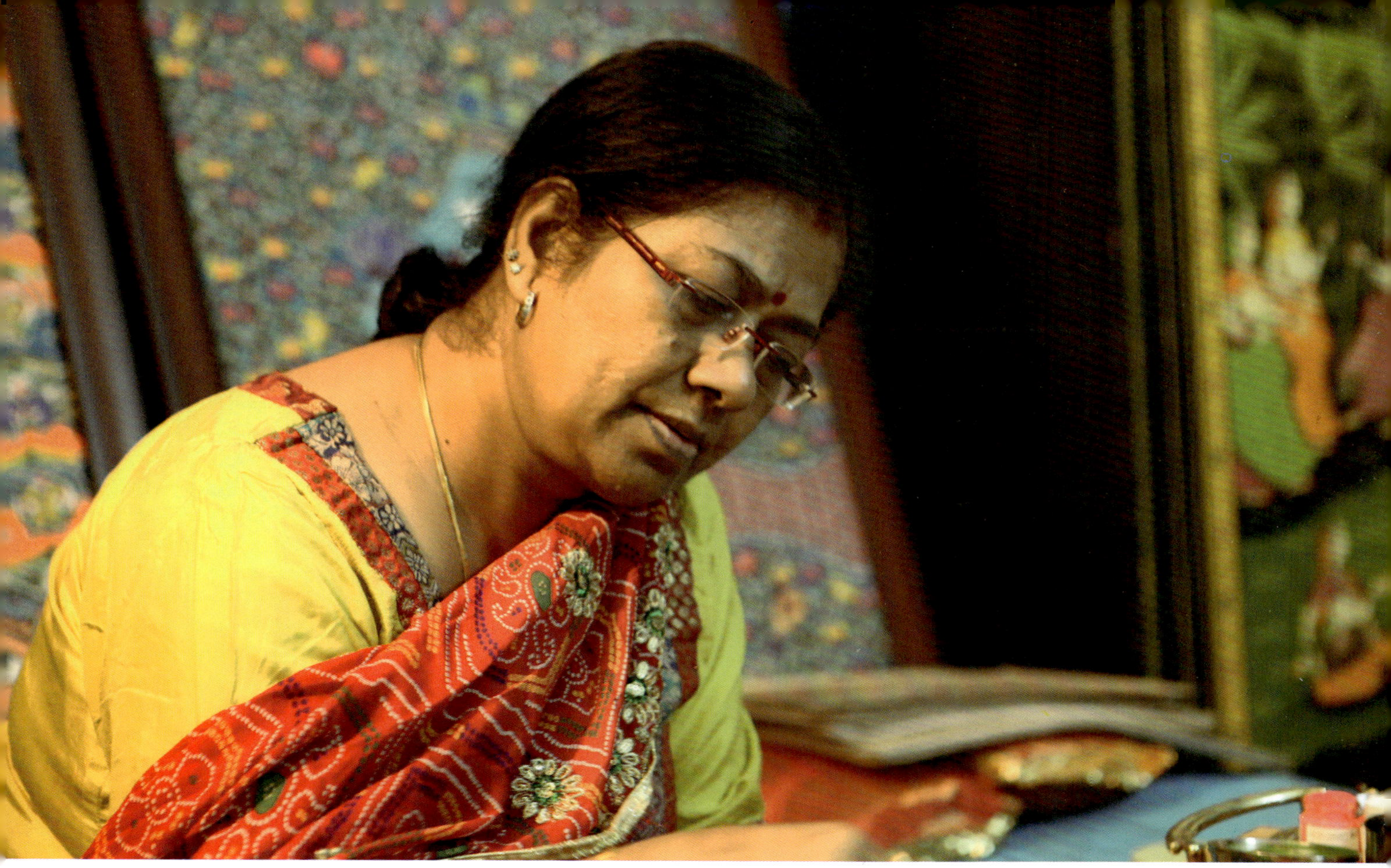

her work. In the mid 1990s, on one of her regular visits to her hometown, she was dismayed to see the art scene there. There was stagnation all around, with men and women churning out repetitive imagery and getting exploited by middlemen for some quick sales in the market. Hence she took it upon herself to help other women artists from her region, guide them to refine their work and sell it through the emporia network in Delhi where she had settled. She did this while continuing and innovating her own artwork.

Managing hearth and home, with two growing children, along with carrying forward her creative engagements was a challenge that Bharti took up with great aplomb. And the first big break came when she was invited to paint the walls and exteriors of Bihar Pavilion at the Indian trade fairgrounds. She has never had to look back. The AIFACS award in 1993, Millennium award in 2001, followed by National and other awards in 2006, plus many others and in quick succession resulted in her getting invited for solo shows in Delhi, and then around the country and the world, putting her career on a firm footing.

Pgs. 8-9: Bharti relaxing at her hometown, Mithila, India. Opposite page: At a temple in Mithila, a woman is putting 'ṭika' on Bharti's forehead. Pgs. 11/12: Bharti is painting in her home studio.

Madhubani Art

The ephemeral folk style know as Madhubani Art is practiced widely in parts of Bihar. Its origin is believed to go back to the ancient era of the Ramayana, when the town was decorated by inhabitants of the region for the wedding of King Janaka's daughter, Sita, to Lord Rama with elaborate Bhitti-Chitra (wall paintings) and murals. Traditionally the art form was known for its five distinctive styles: Bharni, Katchni, Tantrik, Nepali and Gobar/Gohbar. Each style was practised by a particular social group and entailed distinct features, though all retained a uniformity in their focus on the depiction of divinities, rituals, natural elements and daily life. The art style, traditionally a prerogative of the region's women, is undergoing changes in its globalized form today as artists take to newer matter, modes and media for their work.

The philosophy of Madhubani art, a living tradition, is essentially based on the principle of dualism. Opposites run through the form in parallel and in various combinations and permutations: life/death, day/night, joy/sorrow, man/woman, ying/yang and body/soul. They are featured in the imagery to represent a holistic universe. The artscape appears inundated with divine deities (Sita and Rama, Radha and Krishna, Shakti and Shiva), the sun and moon, and flora and fauna along with features found in Buddhism, Islamic Sufism, tantric symbols and classical Hinduism.

Primarily a significant socio-cultural engagement for the womenfolk of Bihar, this art was a welcome break from their daily drudgery. Working together in creating the paintings allowed the women a window to entertain themselves and open up in an otherwise closed society. The collective experience also offered them an opportunity to socialize and share their thoughts and anxieties. In hinterland India, women of the household even today paint walls and floors of their homes to mark special occasions.

However, given its popularity and marketability, men have also taken to the Madhubani style of painting. Well-established procedures are followed to carry forward this living art practice. The surface is first coated with two or three thin layers of mud and cow dung for an auspicious beginning and to bring prosperity into the home. The organic coating also works as a preservative and strengthening agent. The artists then work on the base. They draw the imagery with paste made from powdered rice, and paint with colours extracted from flowers and vegetables, using their fingers, cloth balls, twigs, bamboo pens, and matchsticks. The paintings focus on people and their lives, ancient epics and nature. The sun, the moon, and plants like Tulsi (Basil leaves) are recurring elements, along with village scenes and social events. Hardly any space is left empty. The gaps are filled

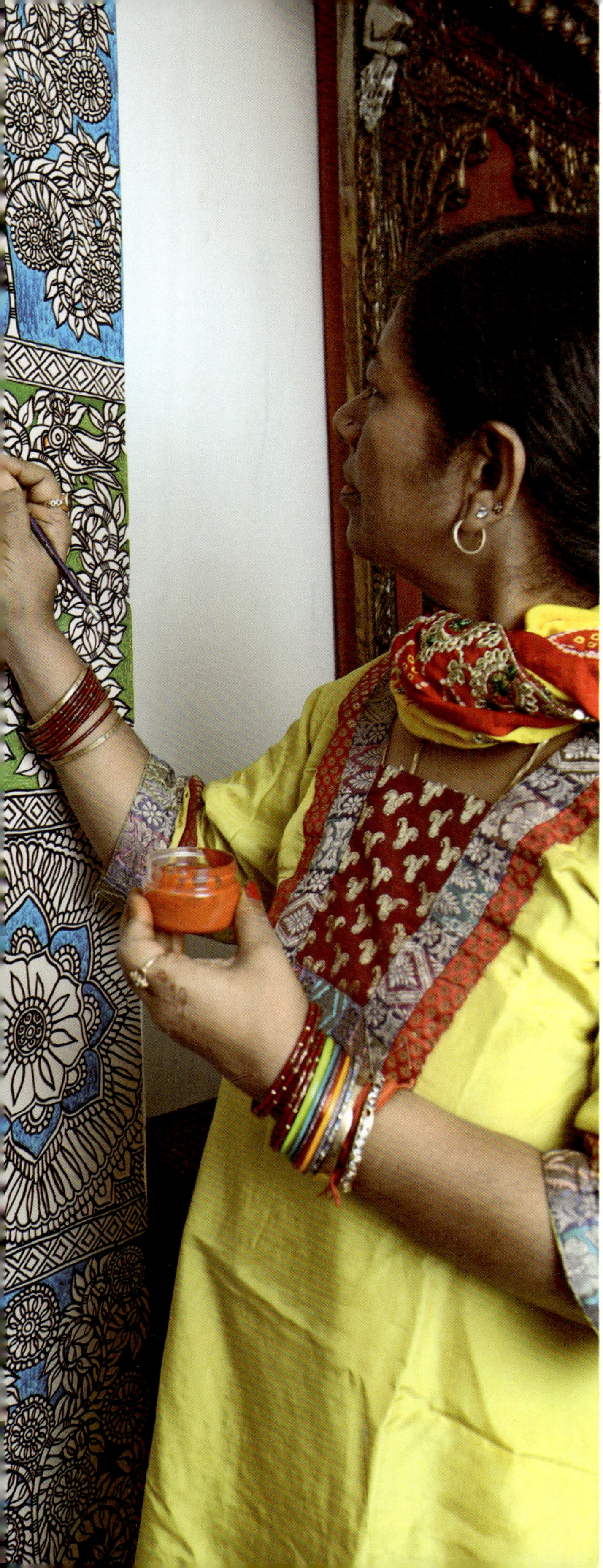

with flowers, animals, birds, and eye-catching geometric patterns and tattoo designs.

Immersed in the folklore of Mithila, fresh forms and figures are painted and repainted for each festival and special occasion, be it childbirth, marriage, Holi (the festival of colours), Diwali (the festival of lights), a special puja (worship) or change of season. Skills and techniques are passed on from one generation to the next, keeping the ephemeral art form and ancestral tradition and its lore alive. Given the readily available, easy to use alternatives, Madhubani artists today are seen to work more with brushes and acrylic paint rather than natural dyes and pigments. They now also work on paper, cloth, canvas and wood to create art and artifacts, besides painting on walls and floors.

Following in the footsteps of the legendary William G. Archer and subsequently Bhaskar Kulkarni and other experts, who brought the art form out of the woods, today significant collections across the world feature fine examples of Madhubani painting. There is a dedicated Mithila Museum in Tokamachi, Japan, which holds around 850 Madhubani paintings. However, work in the popular art style is also getting recycled with so much copying that is beginning to saturate the market. Fortunately, though, there are also some committed artists striving to innovate the tradition and keep it alive.

Mithila is a region of Bihar (India) that's not only rich in art but in architecture as well. Pictured below is Bharti Dayal demonstrating some painting techniques to the women folk-women of this area.

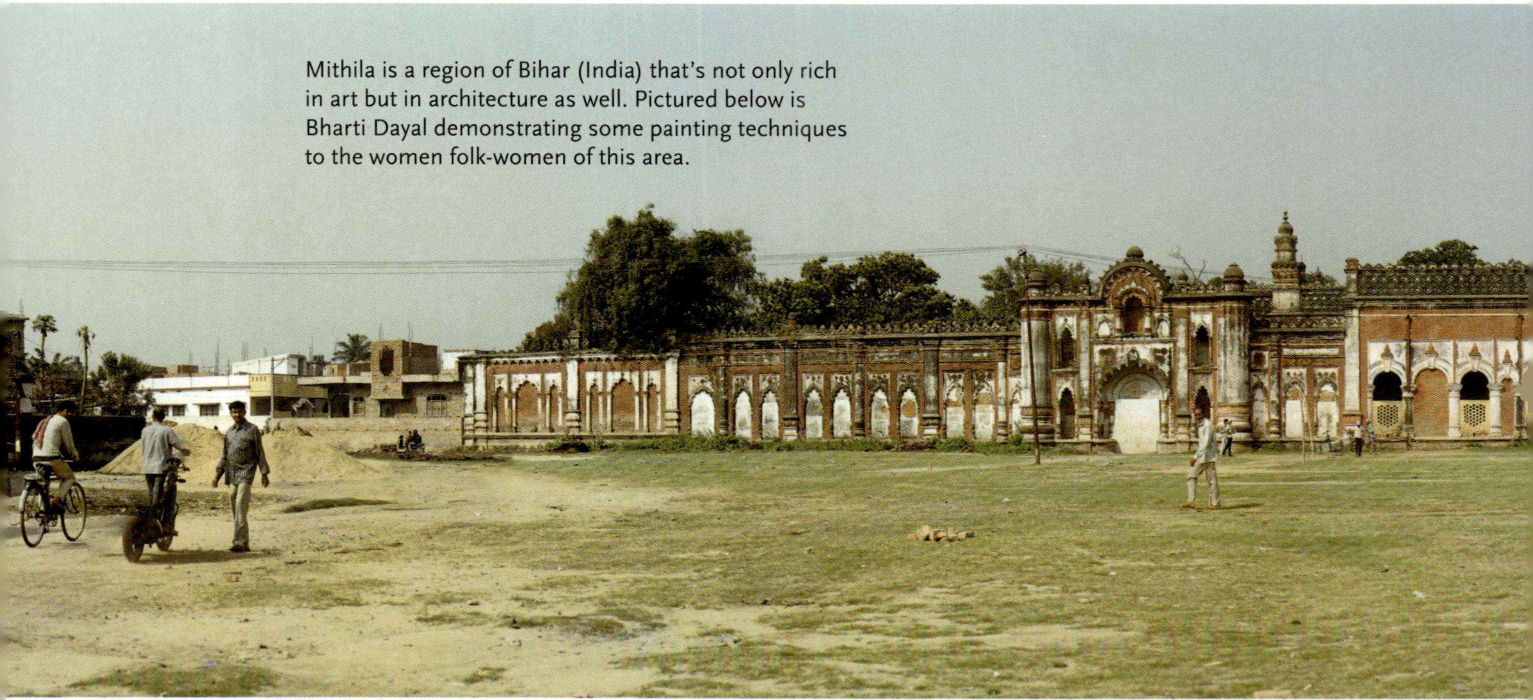

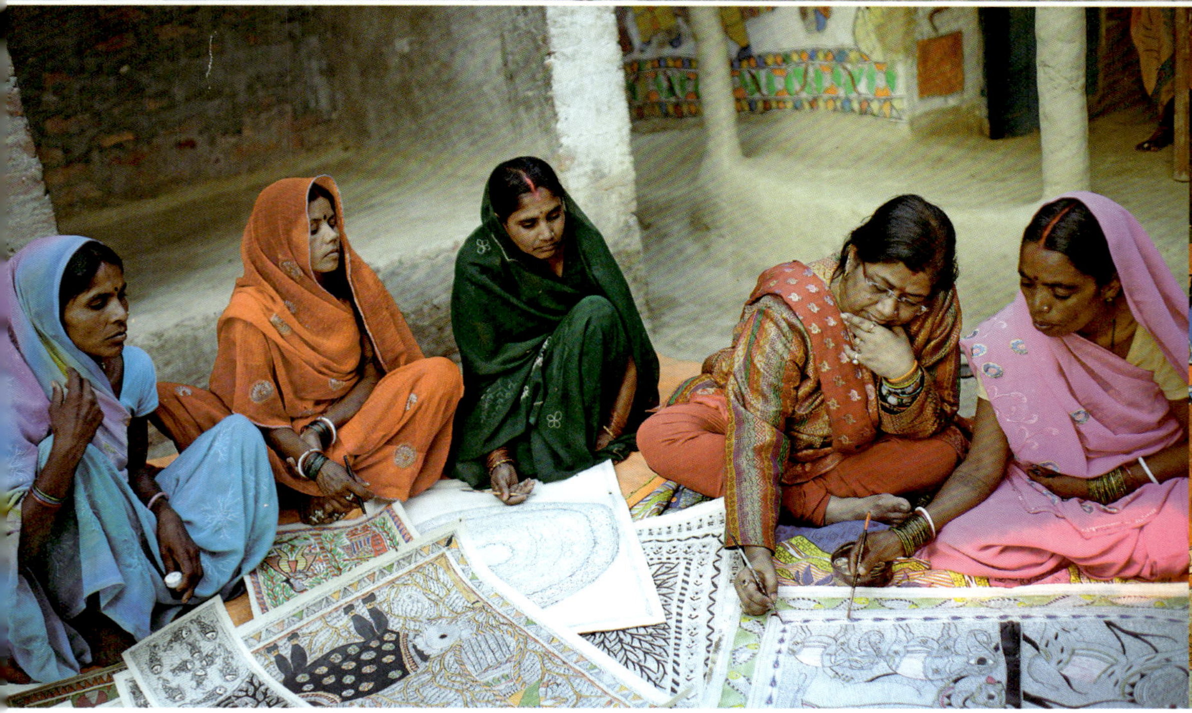

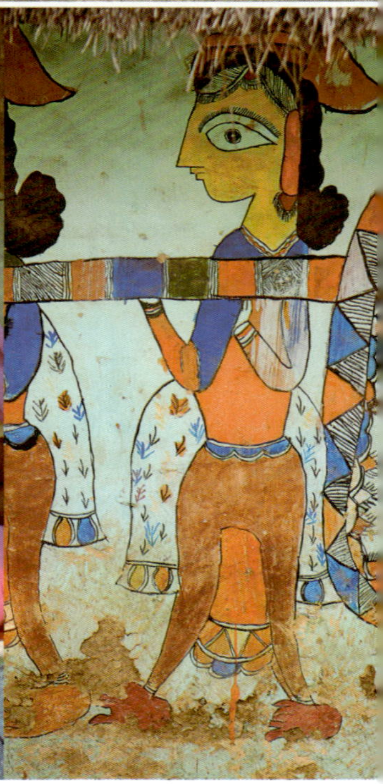

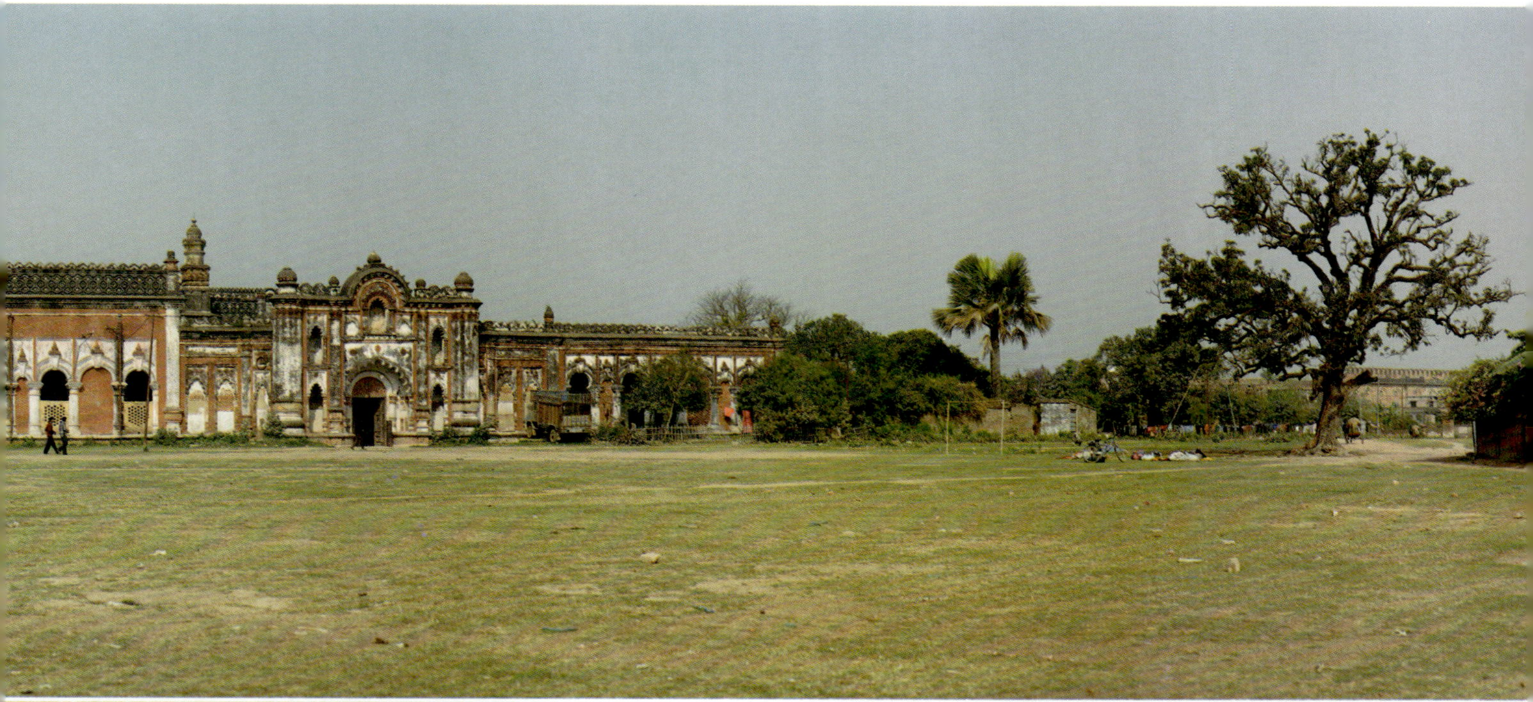
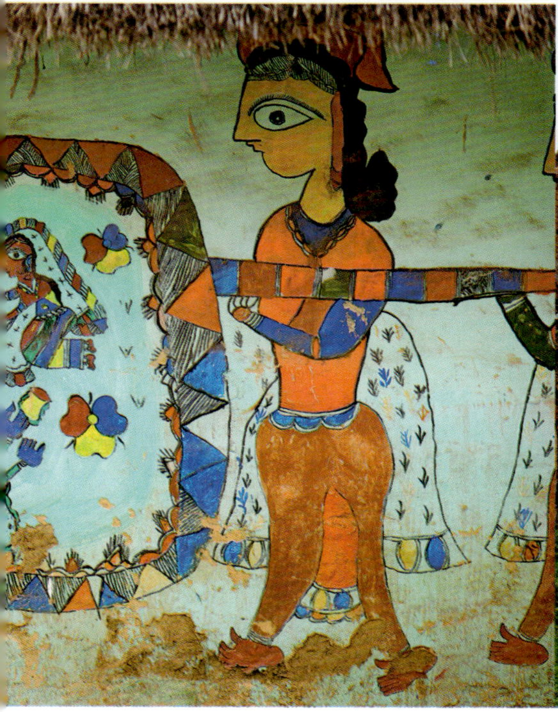
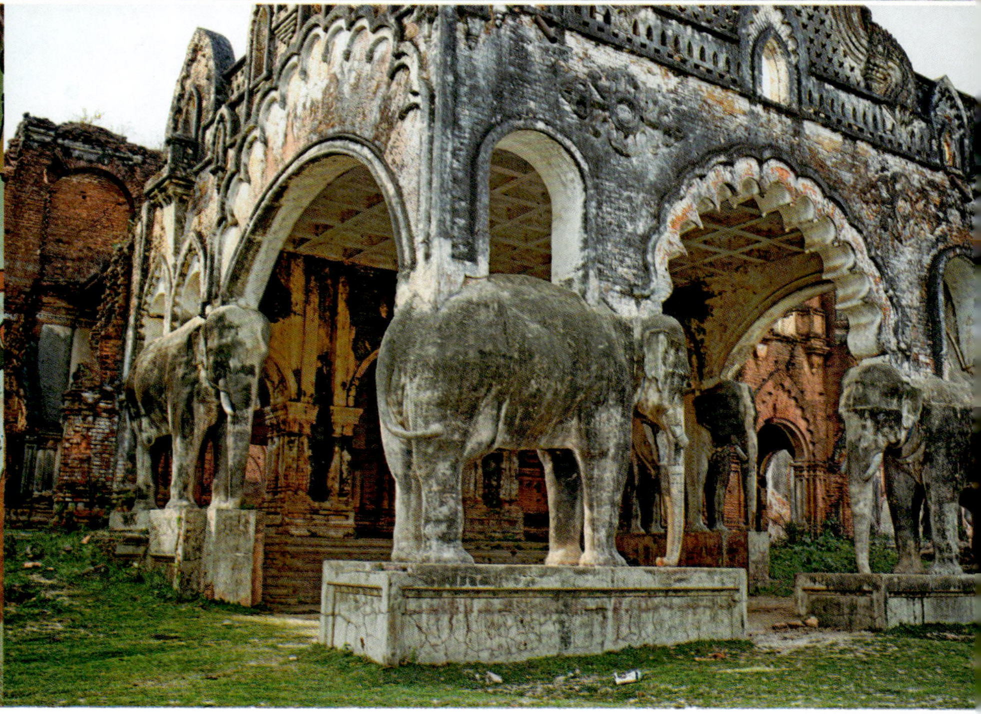

Bharti's Artscape

Bharti Dayal is one such artist who has played a significant role in the re-emergence and propagation of this art form. Meandering through ritual and religious themes, her work features divine icons and epic episodes, besides folklore set amidst picturesque and colourful compositions. In a combination of graphic designs, tatoos, lines, concentric circles, motifs of flora and fauna, spirits and animistic renderings, her paintings entail abstraction along with figurative motifs. Geometric patterns and divine imagery drawn with free abundance come in a rich palette.

Following a strict discipline, Bharti begins to paint only after deciding on the broad theme. But she also allows the initial plan and story to change as the work develops. After preparing the basic sketch on paper or canvas, the imagery is created in freehand as a spontaneous drawing. Pencils and nib pens are used to draw the lines and fill in the details. Vegetable dyes and crushed rice paste are mixed with acrylic. Painting with normal brushes and cotton swabs, she covers the whole surface leaving no space untouched. Several layers of colours are painted one over the other. She uses cotton, silk, canvas and wood in addition to walls as the surface for her art, though much of her work now comes on paper and canvas. The paintings in pigments on handmade paper are done in small sizes, whereas canvases painted in mixed media come in larger format.

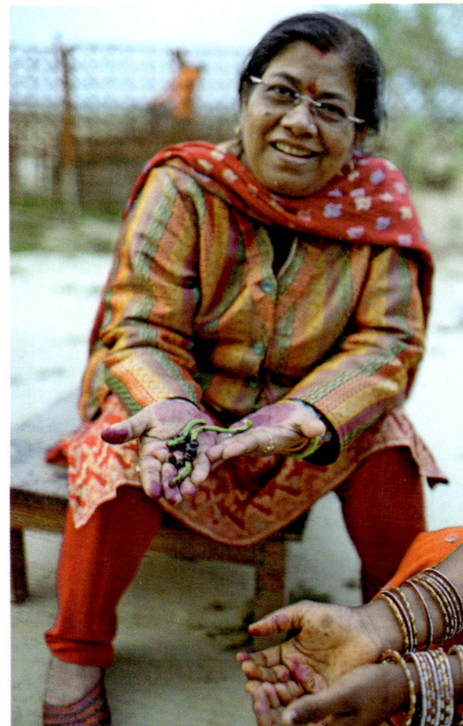

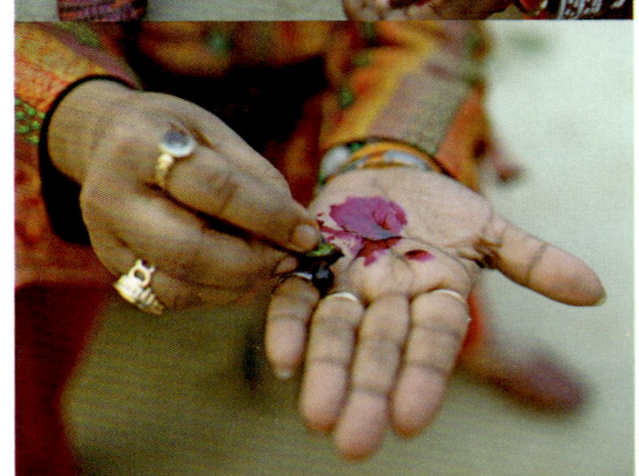

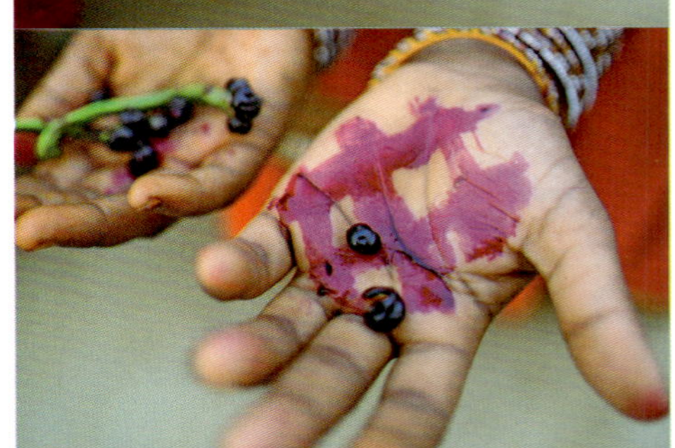

The focal protagonists in her works are the deities worshiped in the region. Figures of adorable Krishna, goddess Shakti, the harbinger of auspicious beginnings Ganesha, the ideal king Rama and other divinities are marked for their prominent nose and fish-shaped eyes with big lashes, stylized features, elaborate hairdos, bangles and other ornamentations. Sacred narratives from the Ramayana are imagined and re-created in intricate details. The beauty of the imagery is enhanced with twirls and swirls. The costumes and jewelry that adorn the icons is drawn in minute detail and painted in measured strokes and not in broad sweeps. The imagery comes soaked in bright reds, blues and greens. Laying her focus on the composition, the artist states, "How you visualize the concept, and what turn you give to the story in the final imagery" all depend on the colours and composition.

Fish, an auspicious sign of growth and prosperity in local folklore, which abound in the region, given the surfeit of ponds every few kilometers, are a recurring feature in Bharti's work. Parrots that signify love and sexuality, and peacocks that suggest romance and devotion appear in her work. There are also bamboo trees and lotus leaves symbolizing fertility and continuation of human life. Rituals re-enacted in graphic presentations, figures invariably shown in profile with languid bodies and elongated noses, and faces as allegories of the sun and the moon are recurring features in Bharti's art. There are geometric patterns and sacred enclosures within the artscape drawn in multiple lines inspired by tantric traditions of the region.

With her knowledge of botany, Bharti is able to experiment with vegetable colours in her work. She creates her own browns with juice extracted from banana, recycles fallen seeds and flowers to extract greens and reds, and her ink comes from the lampblack. Organic extracts are mixed with acrylic colours in her palette, marked for its subtle tones. Innovative in spirit, Bharti likes to play around with the palette to endow her work with the desired ambience. Turquoise blue is a colour that she is increasingly using in her work now, as red replaces the pink that she says "though signifying auspiciousness, also suggests aggression and passion". Green, associated with sex and greed as well as nature, is a much-used colour in her art, as is blue to suggest peace. White in blank spaces adds a meditative element to the work. And eyes are drawn last of all to infuse life into the form.

Care is taken to encompass elements and themes connected with a new generation besides divine icons. Her compositions painted in Madhubani style engage with contemporary socio-cultural issues such as her painting of a girl child, which appeared as the cover for a book on the changing face of the Indian economy. The images of birds on trees recall her childhood memories and emotions. The work made on handmade paper is rooted in the soil and "is linked to my culture" and then taken to new heights with infusion of fresh elements including new materials, tools and colours.

The artist starts her day with a couple of hours of puja in the morning. A cup of tea follows, but no breakfast, and then painting until lunchtime, then back again into the studio corner at home to paint, with mantras and classical music playing in the background. Evenings are kept aside for meetings and visits. Late evenings and dinner time is spent with the family and the day ends with painting for a couple of hours more. A visit to the Kalka Devi temple in Delhi in the vicinity of her home late at night is another regular fixture in her daily schedule. Bharti's days are long allowing her just 5 to 6 hours of sleep on average.

In terms of subjects, Bharti's art rotates around the devotional, sacred and spiritual linking the old with the new. The divine mythical characters that figure in her art are not hemmed in by tradition. They are individuals striving for sublimity. There are undercurrents of longing and peace in her renditions of Radha and Krishna. Their playful acts and Raas Leela form a significant part of the artist's repository. It is to Krishna that she turns at difficult moments. "He is there in my work as my philosopher and friend, not just a visual element." Imaging and painting the divine couple "gives me a sense of completeness", declares the artist.

A believer in the cycle of life and theory of karma and dharma, or "as you sow so shall you reap," she puts her heart and soul into what she paints. Her compositions come with philosophical underpinnings and a refreshing feel. The work assimilates folk imprints, in rhythm with this day and age. She has painted a series of Shiva and Shakti as well as Ardhanarishwara (half-man half-female form). The divine ecstasy of the Tandava dance of Shiva is reflected in her earthy representation of the divine form. Saraswati and Aadishakti and other demigods adulated in the region also figure in her lively and colourful canvases, conveying intricate stories filled with emotion, intrigue, mystery, and symbolism.

Bharti has also painted something traditionally seen as the prerogative of a particular marginalised social group of Bihari women: the elaborate kohbar, or nuptial chamber during weddings, with moon and sun, tortoise and snake, lotus and bamboo tree as symbols of male and female genitalia. Navgraha (the nine planets) as signs of the cosmos bestow love, prosperity and fertility on the newlyweds.

Bharti's elaborately painted divine imagery in Madhubani style also engages with organic forms, folklore, local flora-fauna as well as bestiary imagery and oral history. Her deities imagined and composed in bold figuration based on traditional tattoo patterns help bridge the divide between art and crafts and add to the

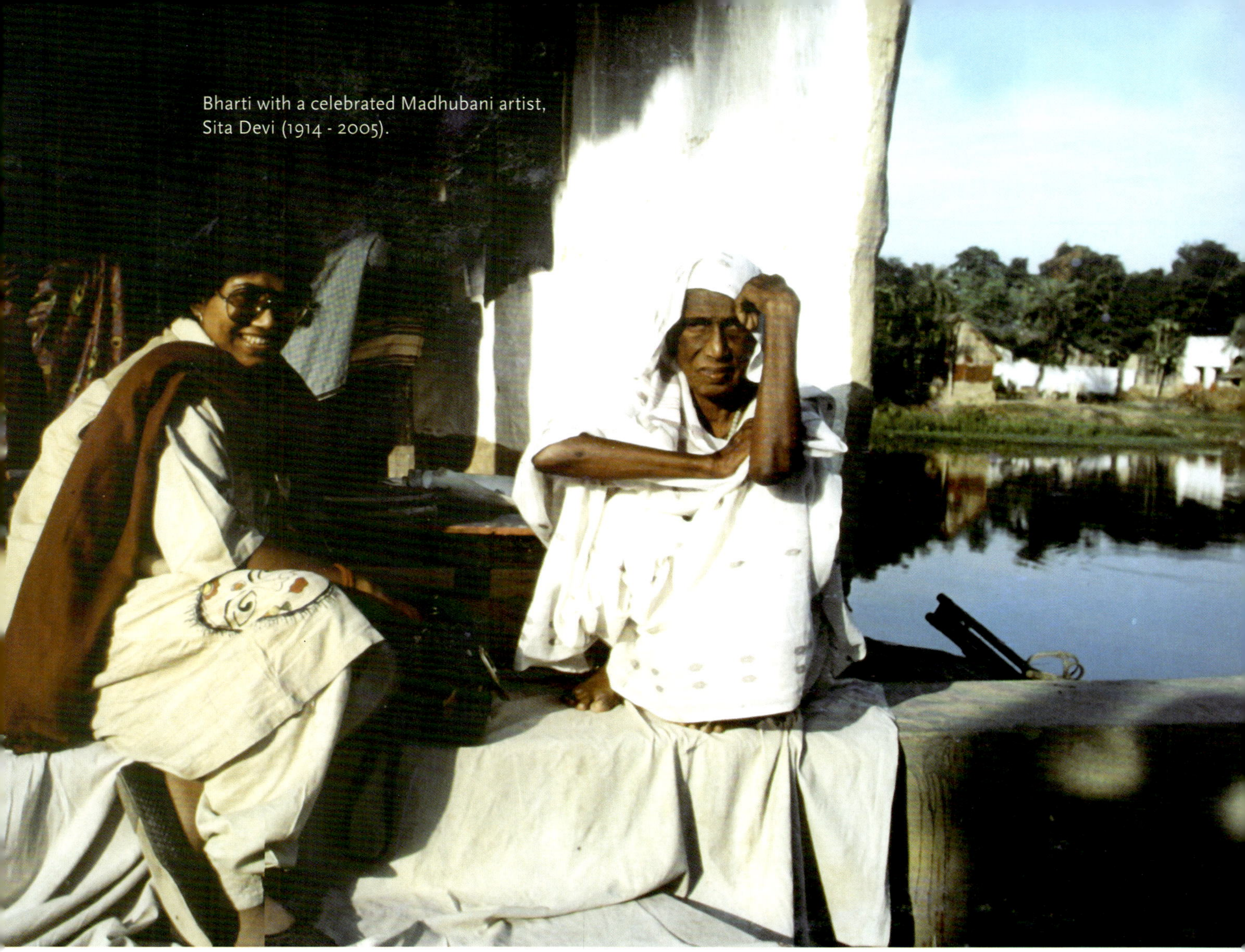

Bharti with a celebrated Madhubani artist, Sita Devi (1914 - 2005).

distinctive art style flourishing in the region. A winner of numerous honours and awards, she has included contemporary elements and an intellectual edge in her work. A vigorous proponent of Madhubani art, she stands tall in the list of famous Mithila painters along with the late Ganga Devi and the late Sita Devi (Pictured above). Her work, shown professionally since 1991, has been documented by French television and the Discovery Channel.

In a unique assimilation of the tradition and modernity, her work contains a fresh and graceful look that appeals to a wider and global audience. She is aptly credited for bringing Madhubani art onto the fine art pedestal and not having it treated as a simplistic folk/craft form.

The text in quotes is based on the writer's conversations with the artist.

Krishna

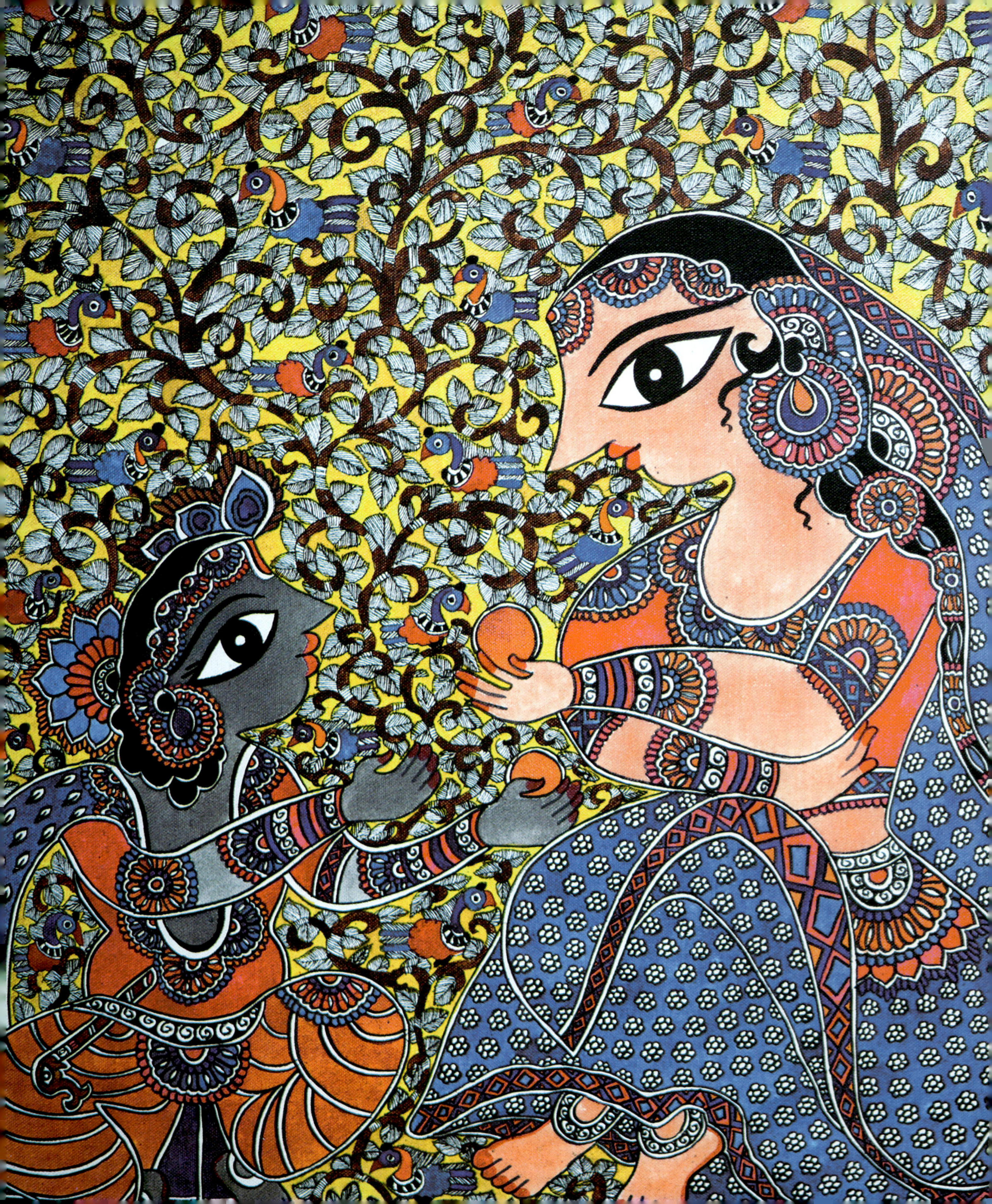

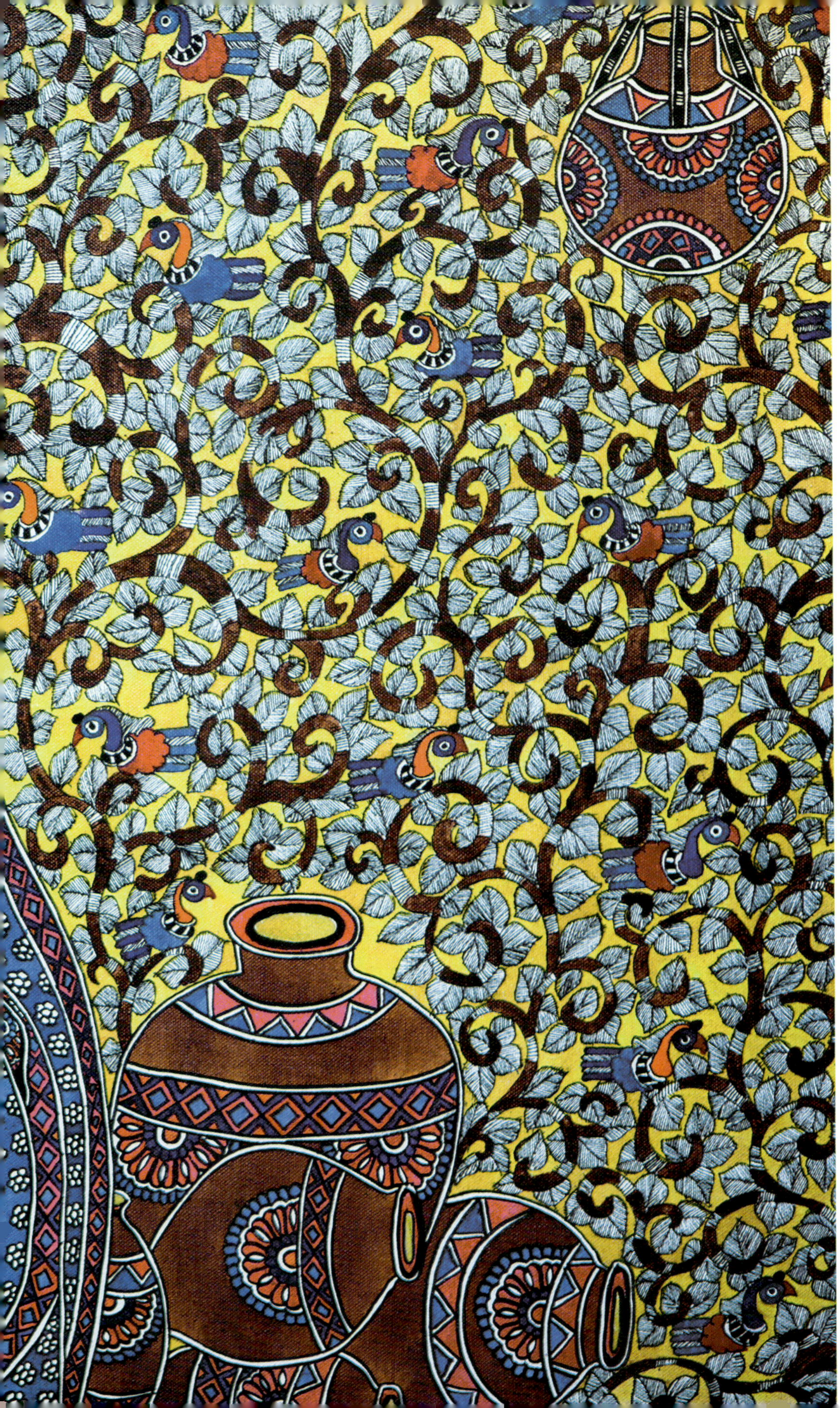

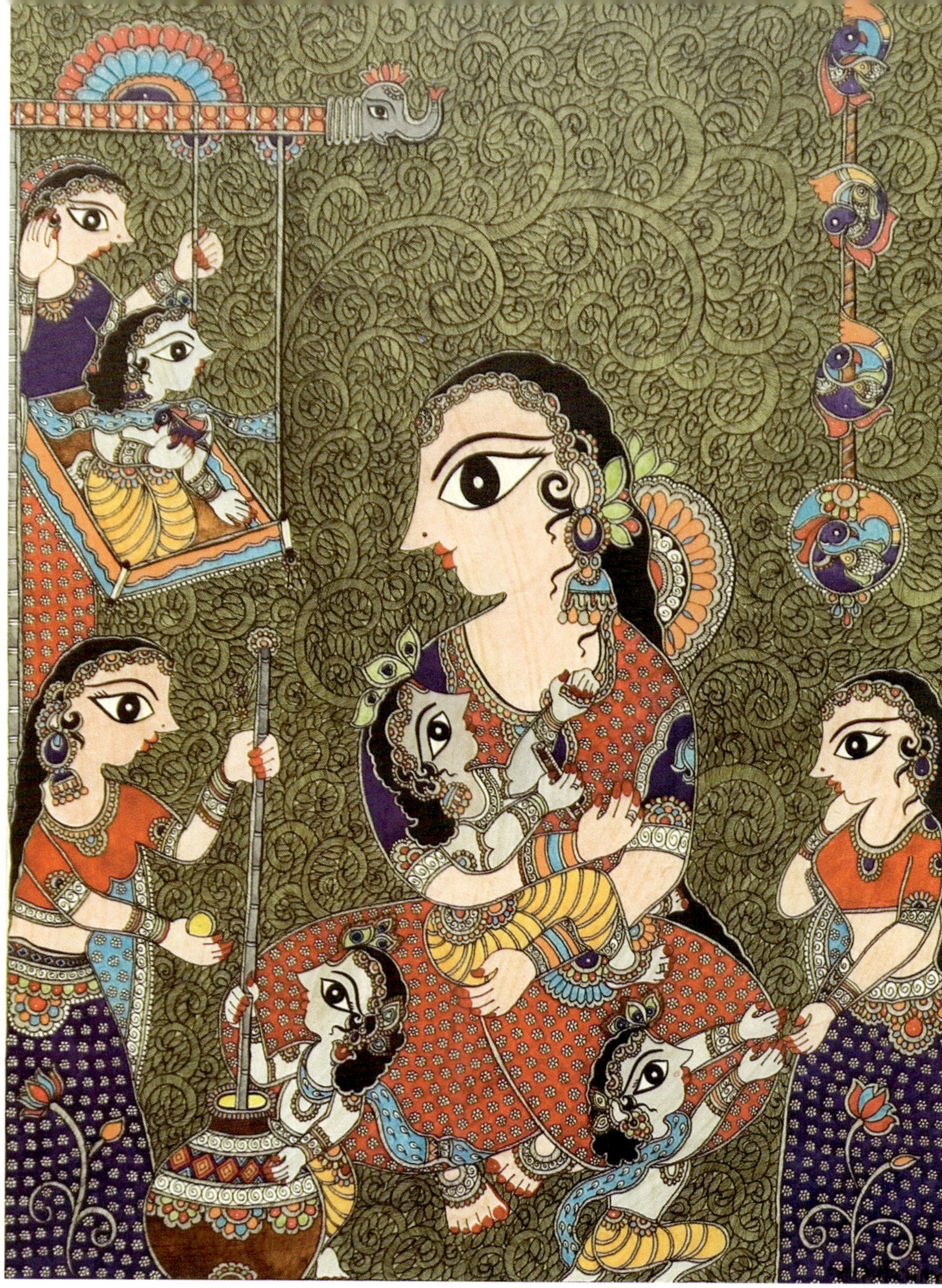

Mother Yashoda Holding Baby Krishna
Pigments on Paper, 75 x 56 cm

Krishna Dancing on Kaliya
Acrylic on Canvas, 100 x 70 cm (p. 25)

Mother Yashoda Feeding Baby Krishna
Acrylic on Canvas, 95 x 68 cm (p. 22-23)

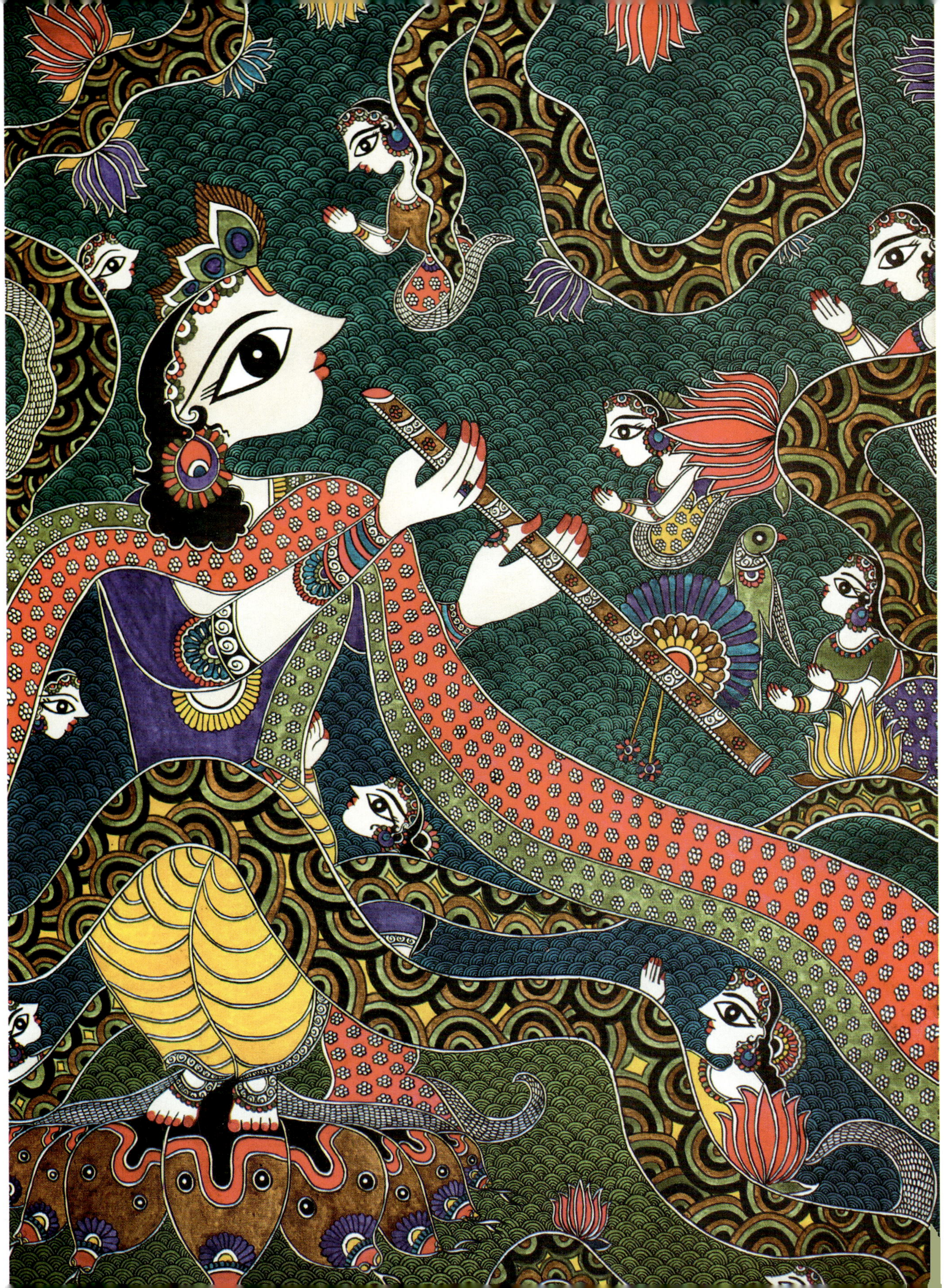

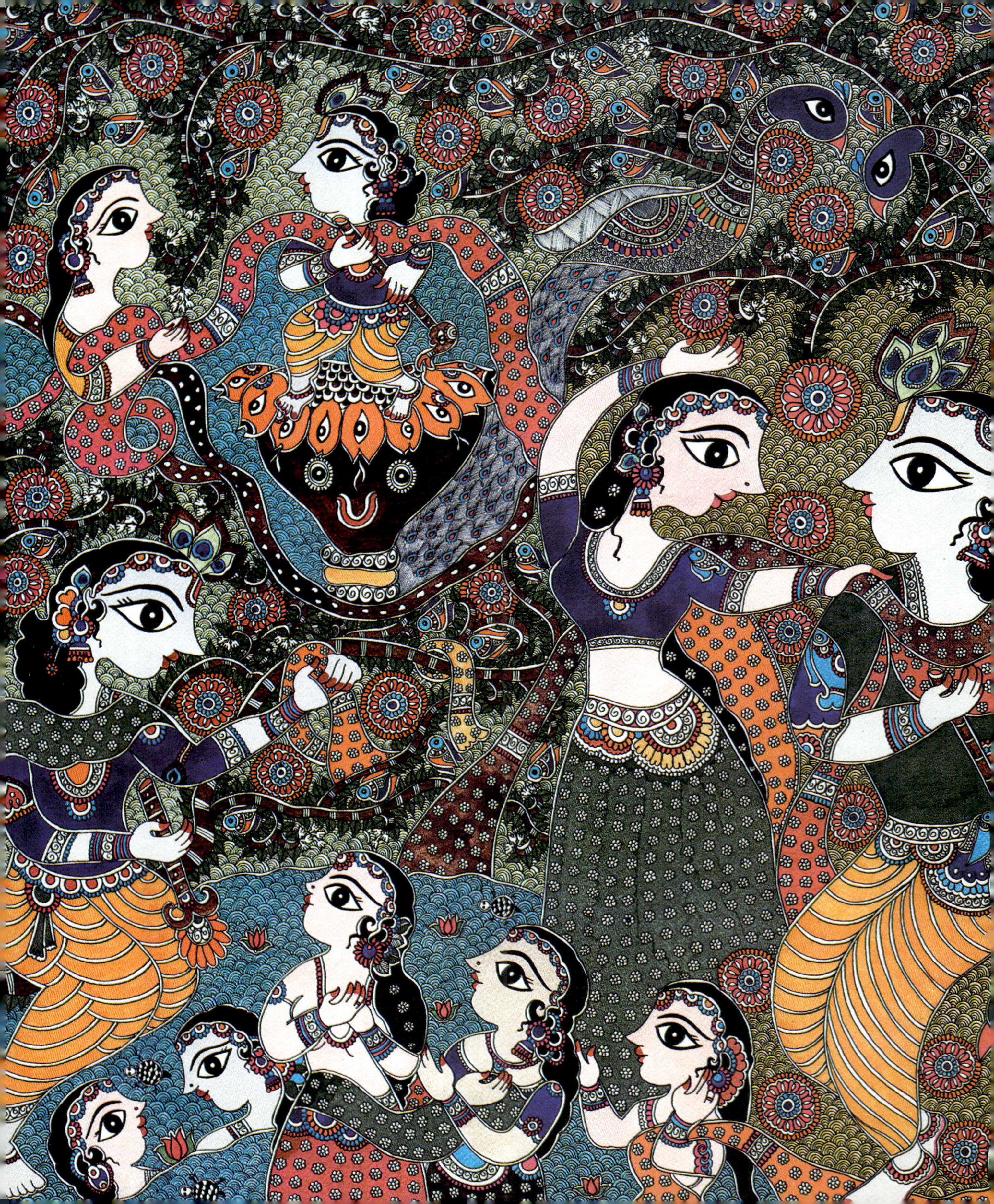

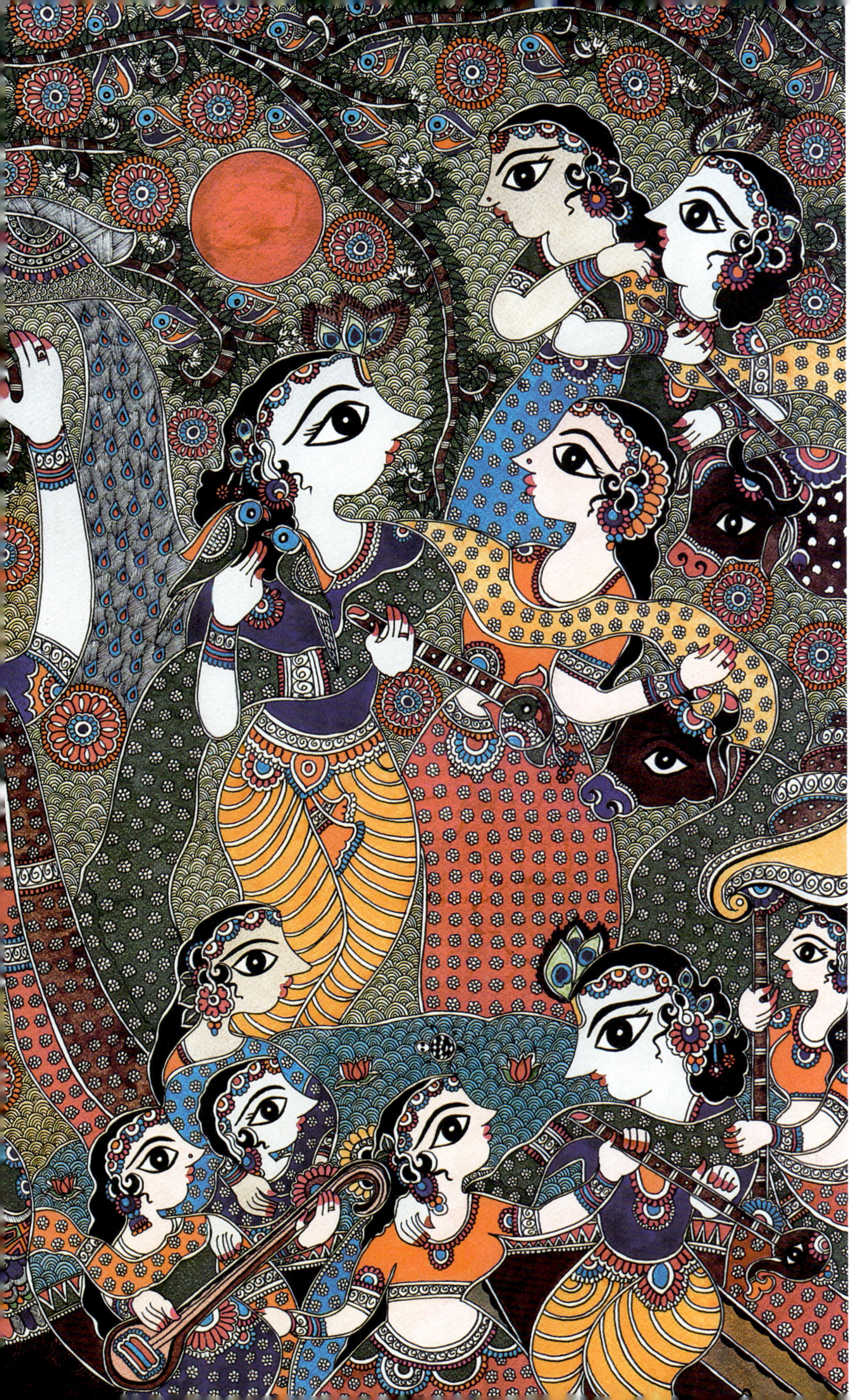

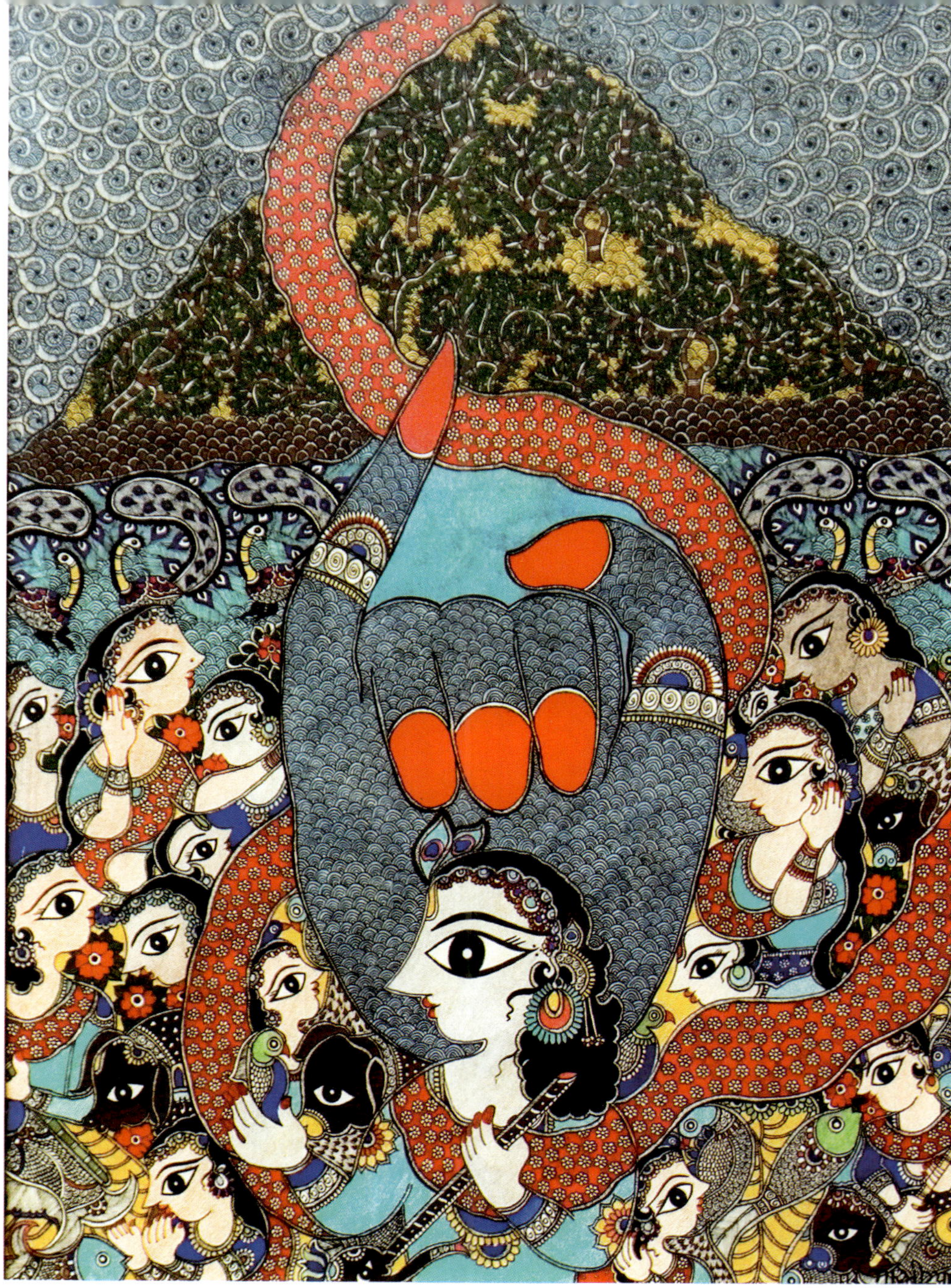

Krishna Lifting Govardhana Hill (I)
Pigments on Paper, 73 x 53 cm

Krishna Lifting Govardhana Hill (II)
Pigments on Paper, 56 x 37 cm (p. 29)

Krishna Dancing on Kaliya and Other Pastimes
Pigments on Paper, 70 x 102 cm (pp. 26–27)

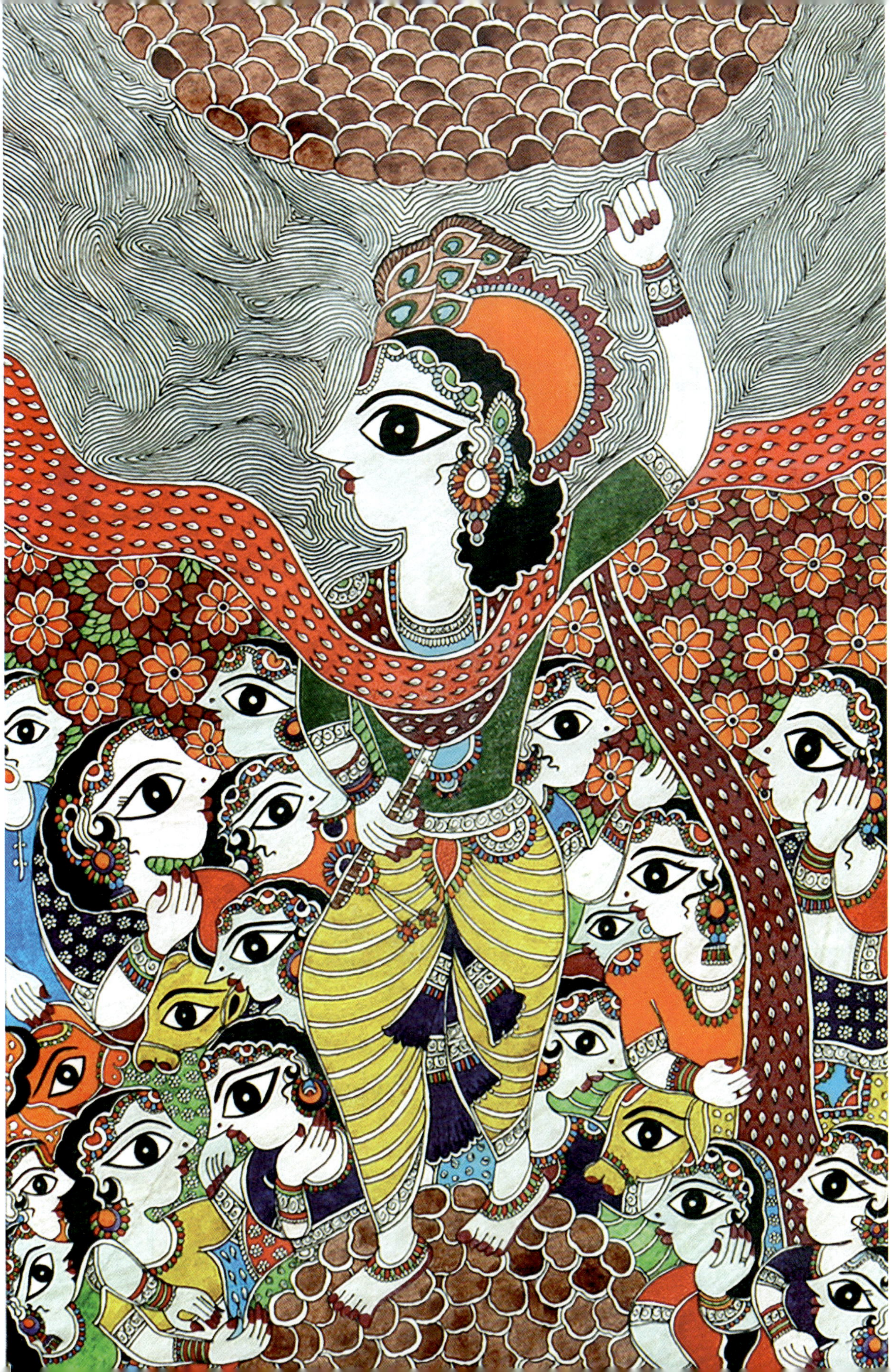

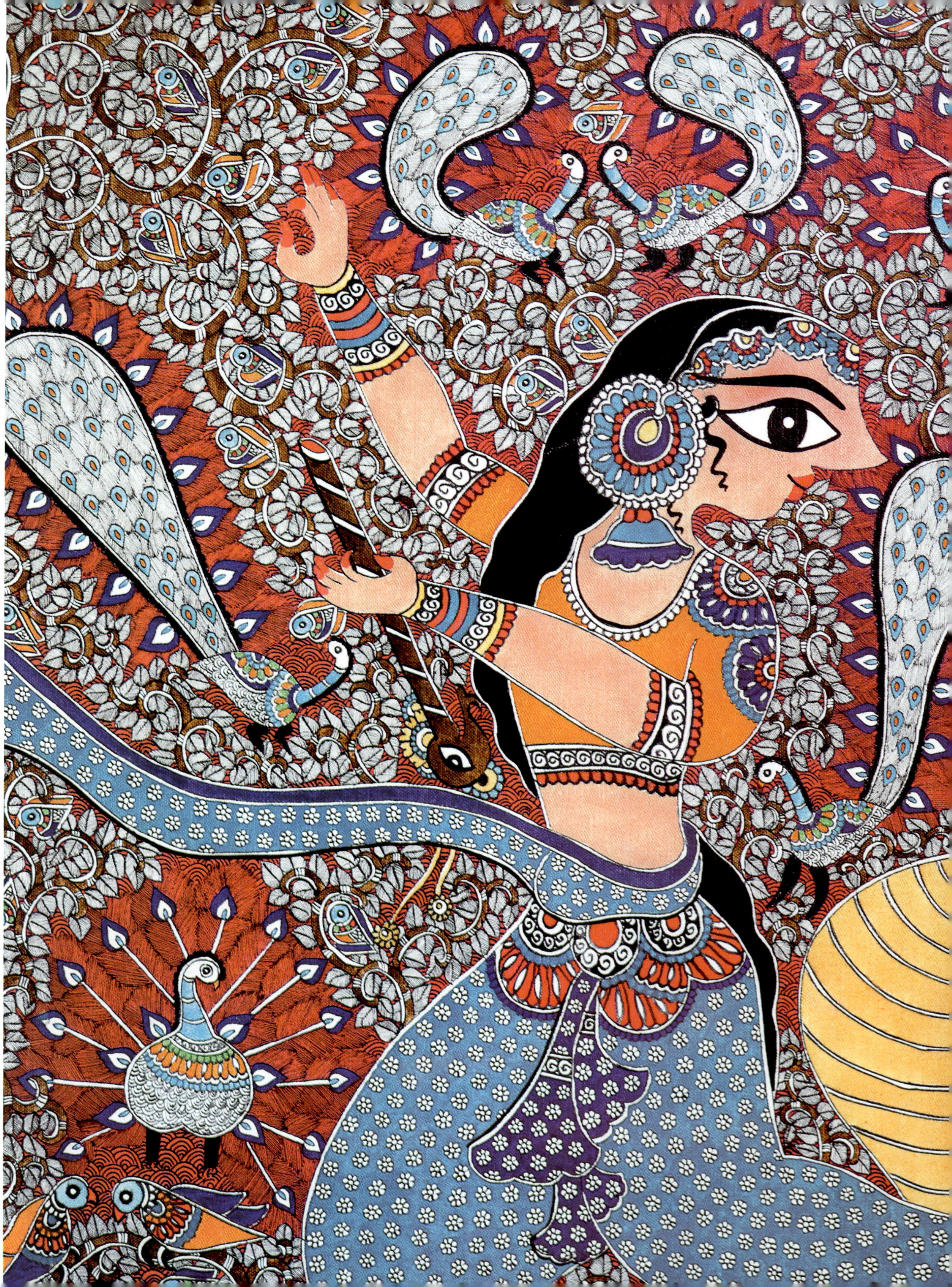

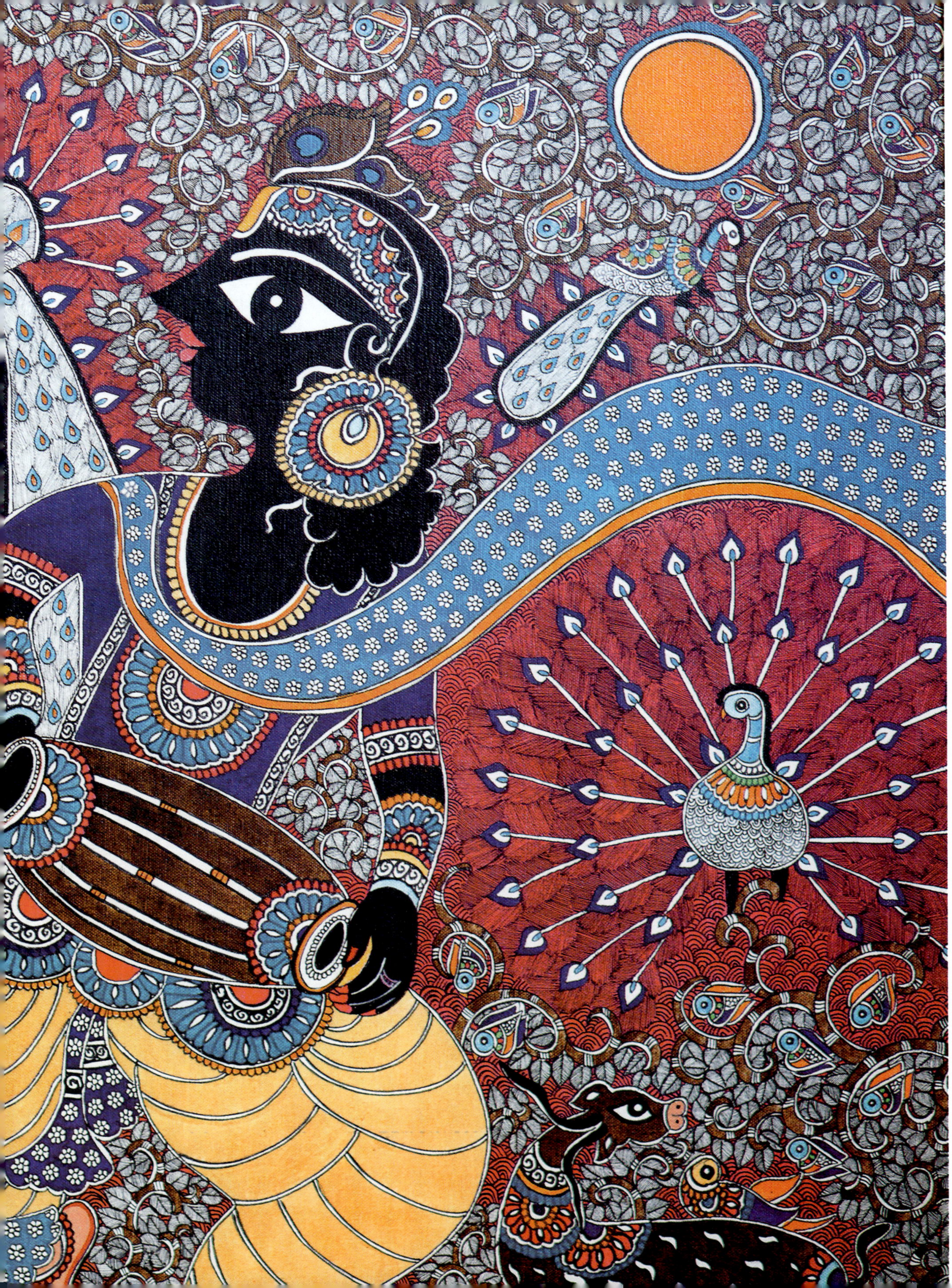

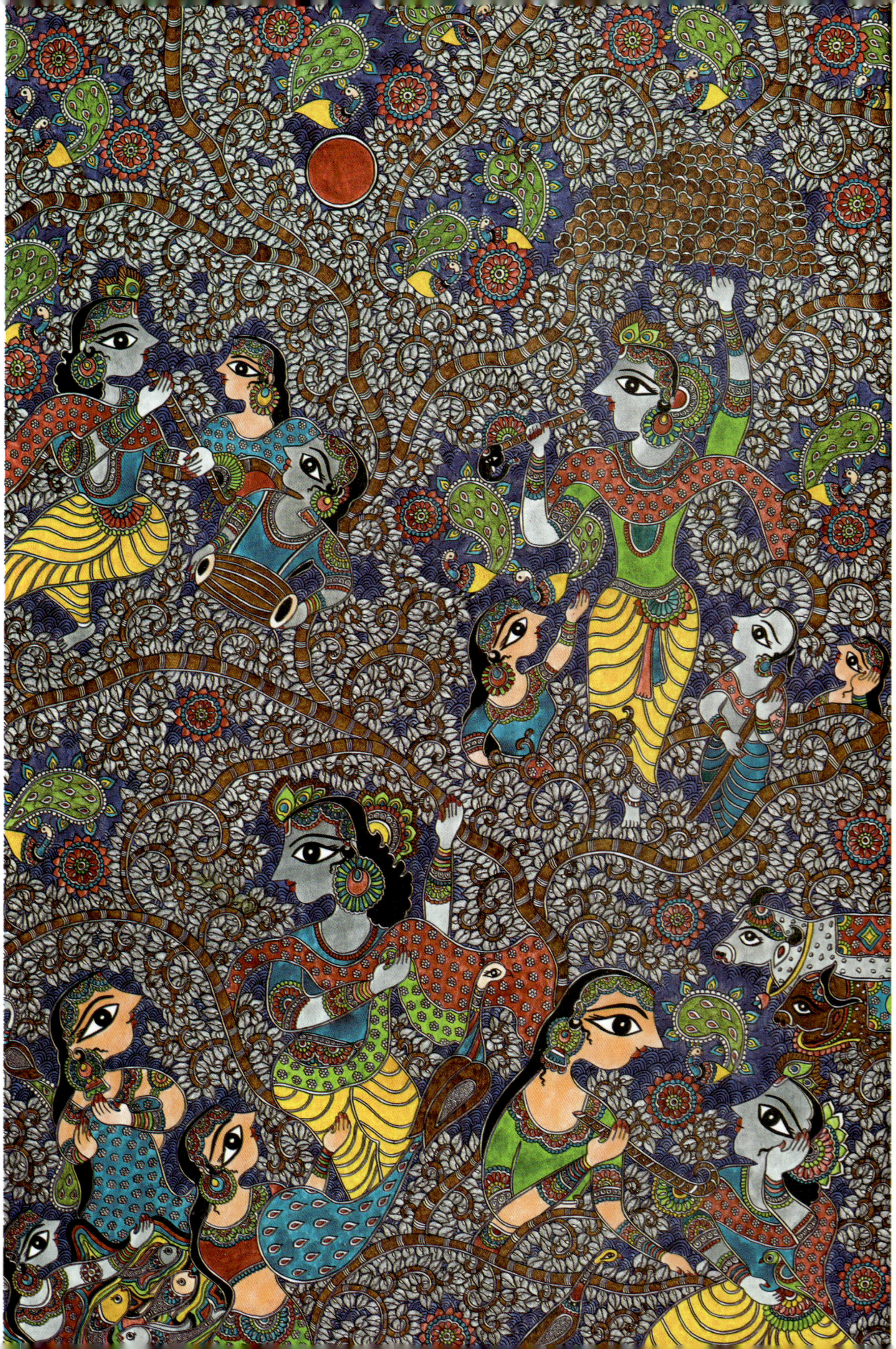

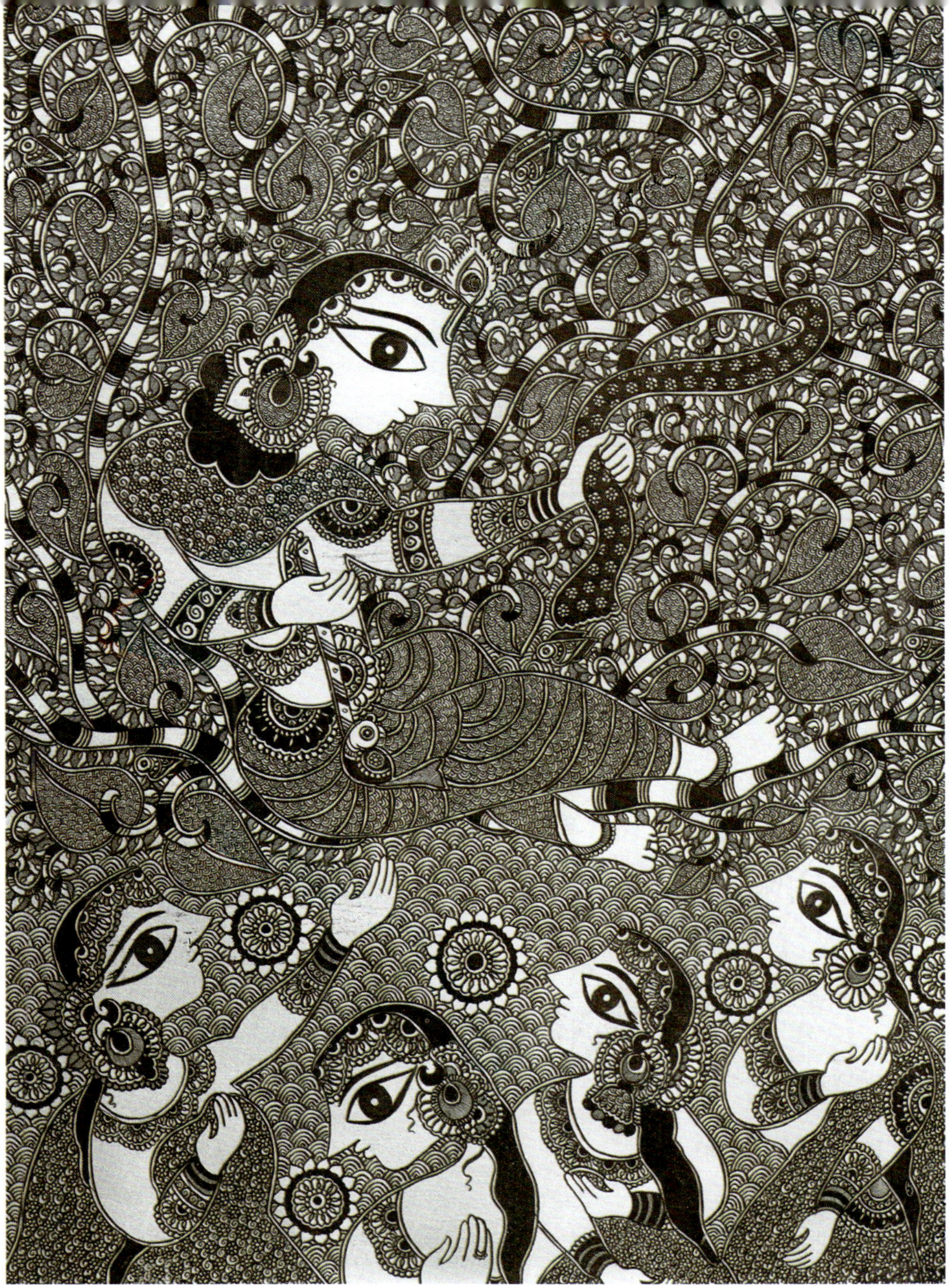

Krishna Steals Gopi Saris
Acrylic on Canvas, 93 x 68 cm

Krishna Lifting Gorvadhana and Other Pastimes
Acrylic on Canvas, 142 x 90 cm (p. 32)

Radha-Krishna Playing Mrdanga and Flute
Acrylic on Canvas, 71 x 96 cm (pp. 30-31)

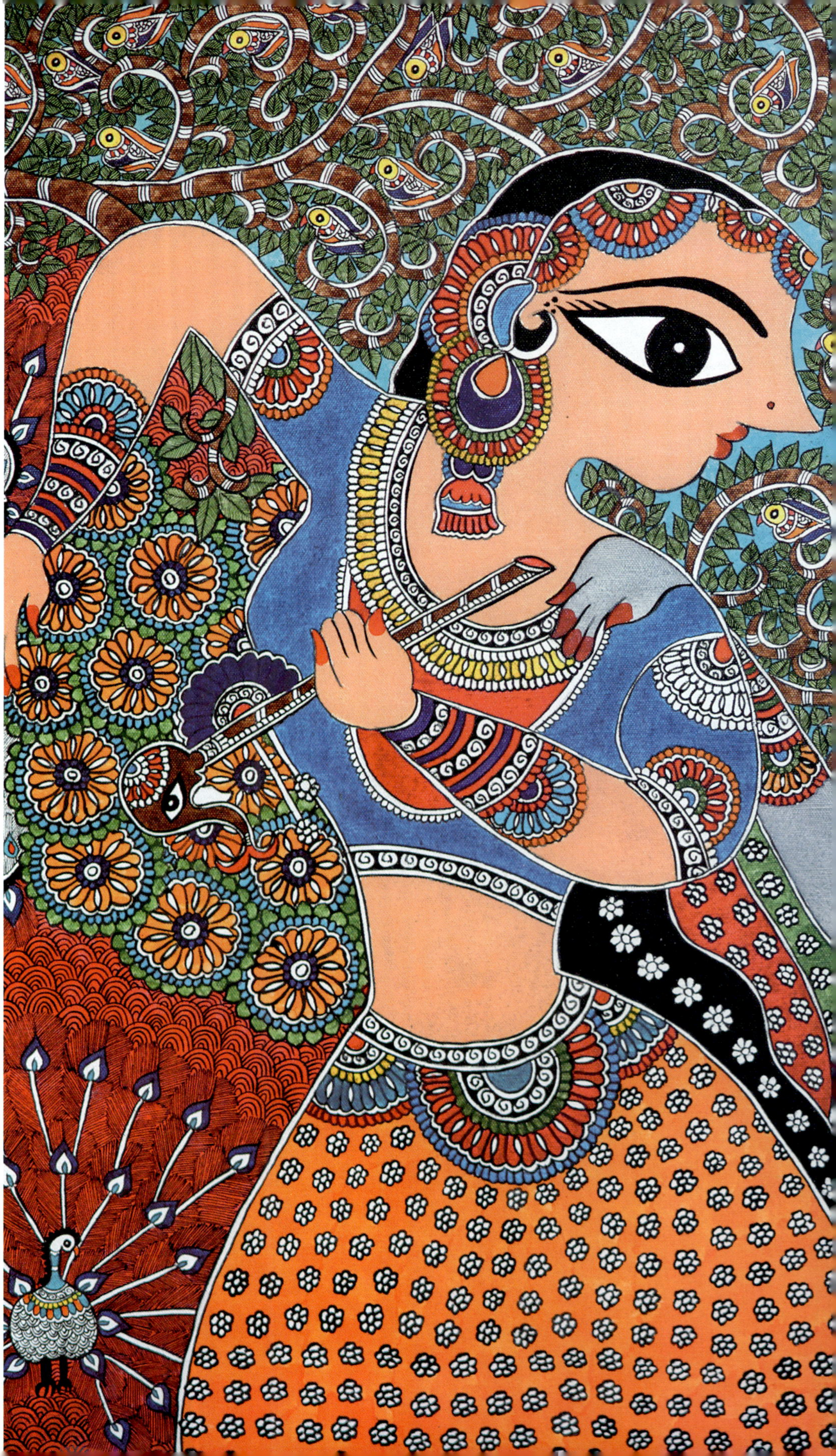

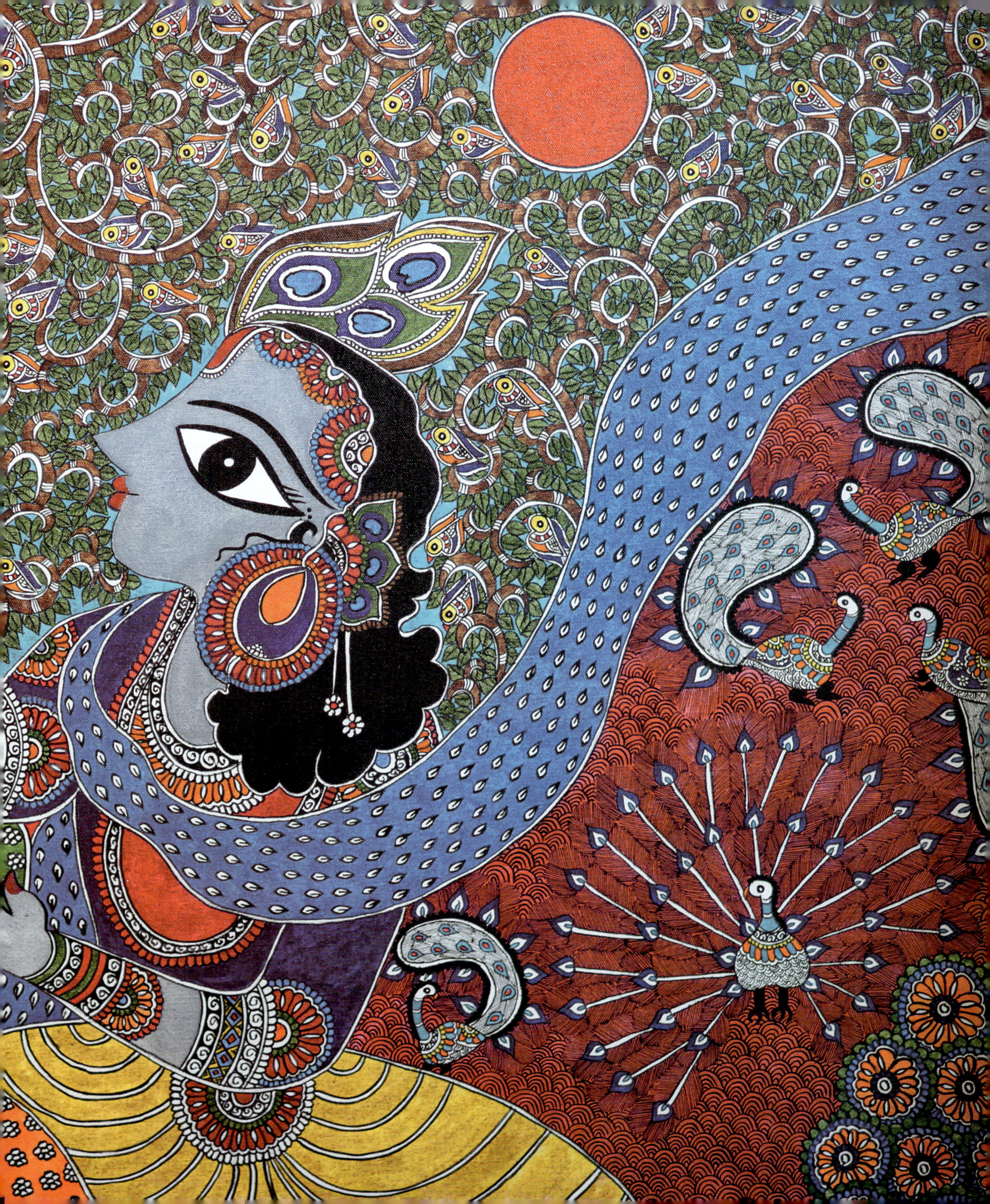

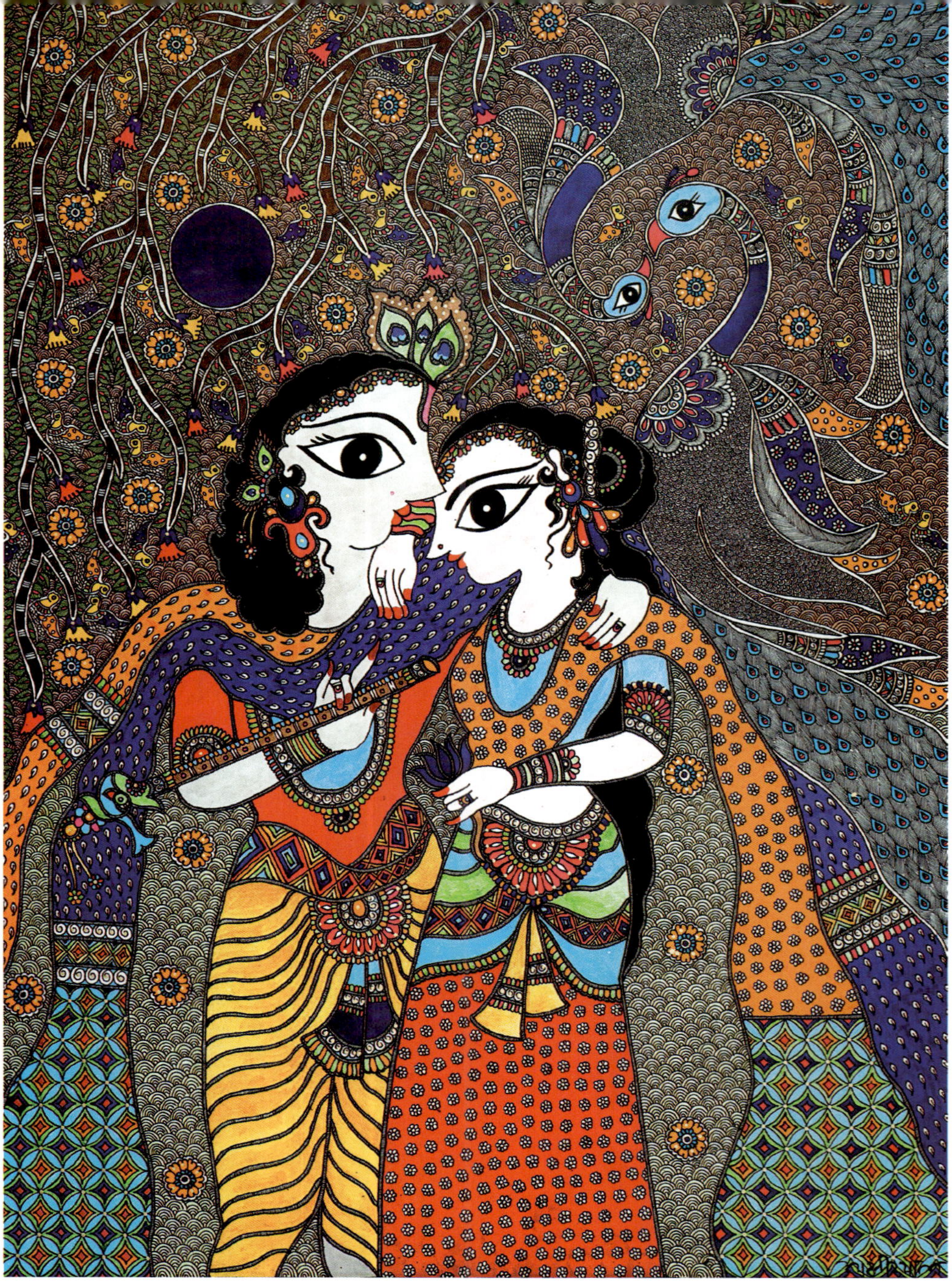

Radha-Krishna Alone with Peacocks
Pigments on Paper, 75 x 55 cm

Krishna with Gopis and Cows
Pigments on Paper, 75 x 55 cm (p. 37)

Radha-Krishna with Flute
Acrylic on Canvas, 77 x 92 cm (pp. 34-35)

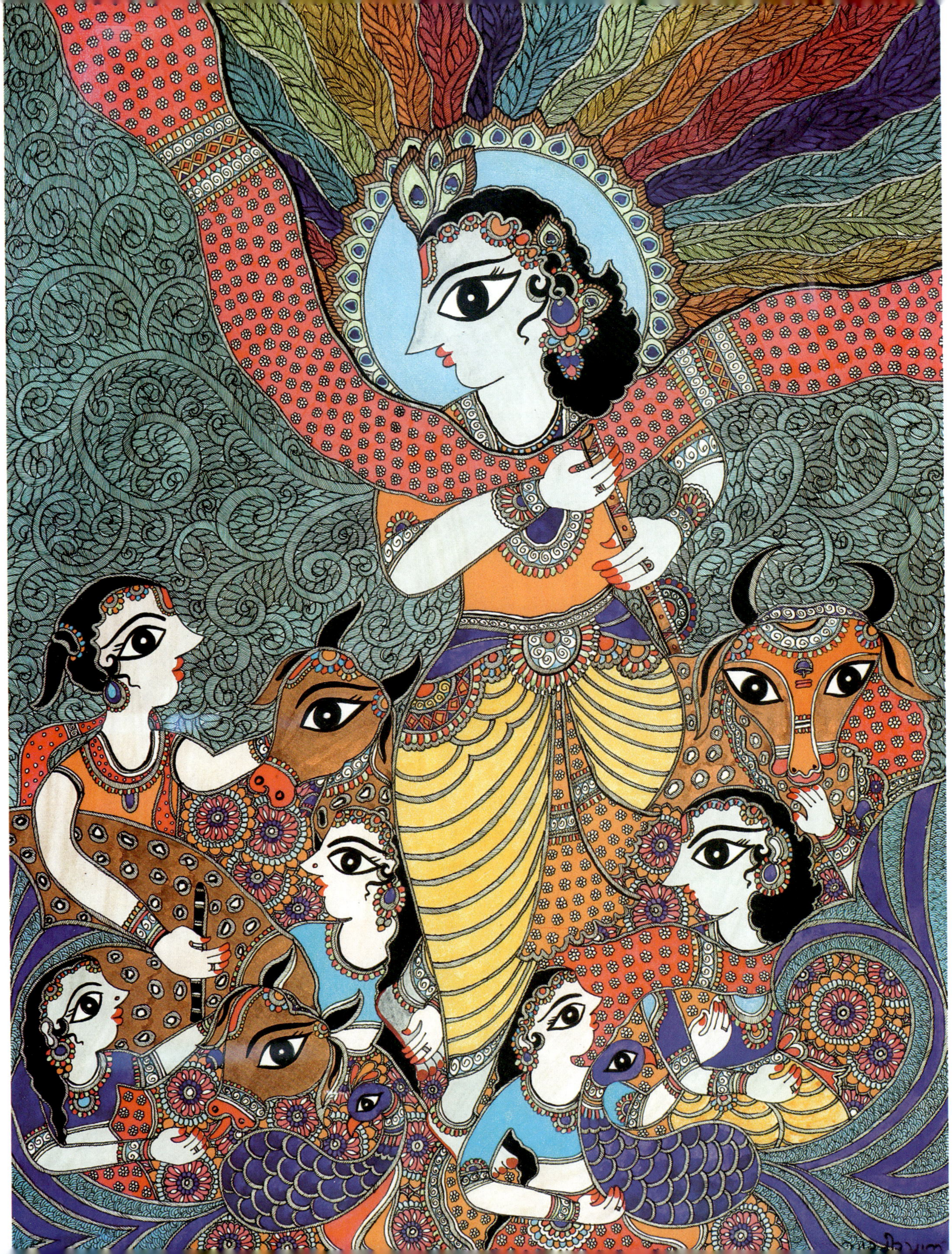

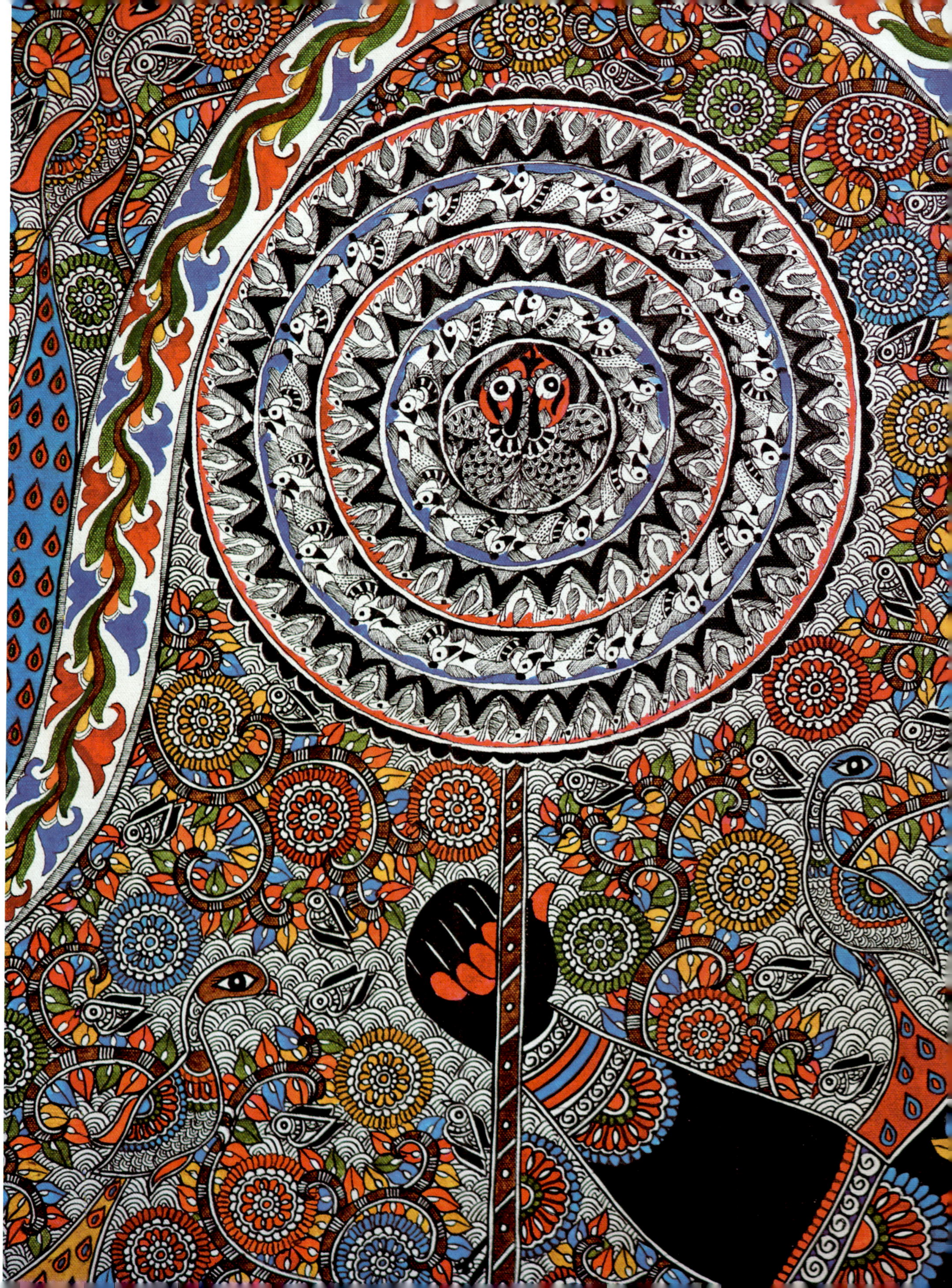

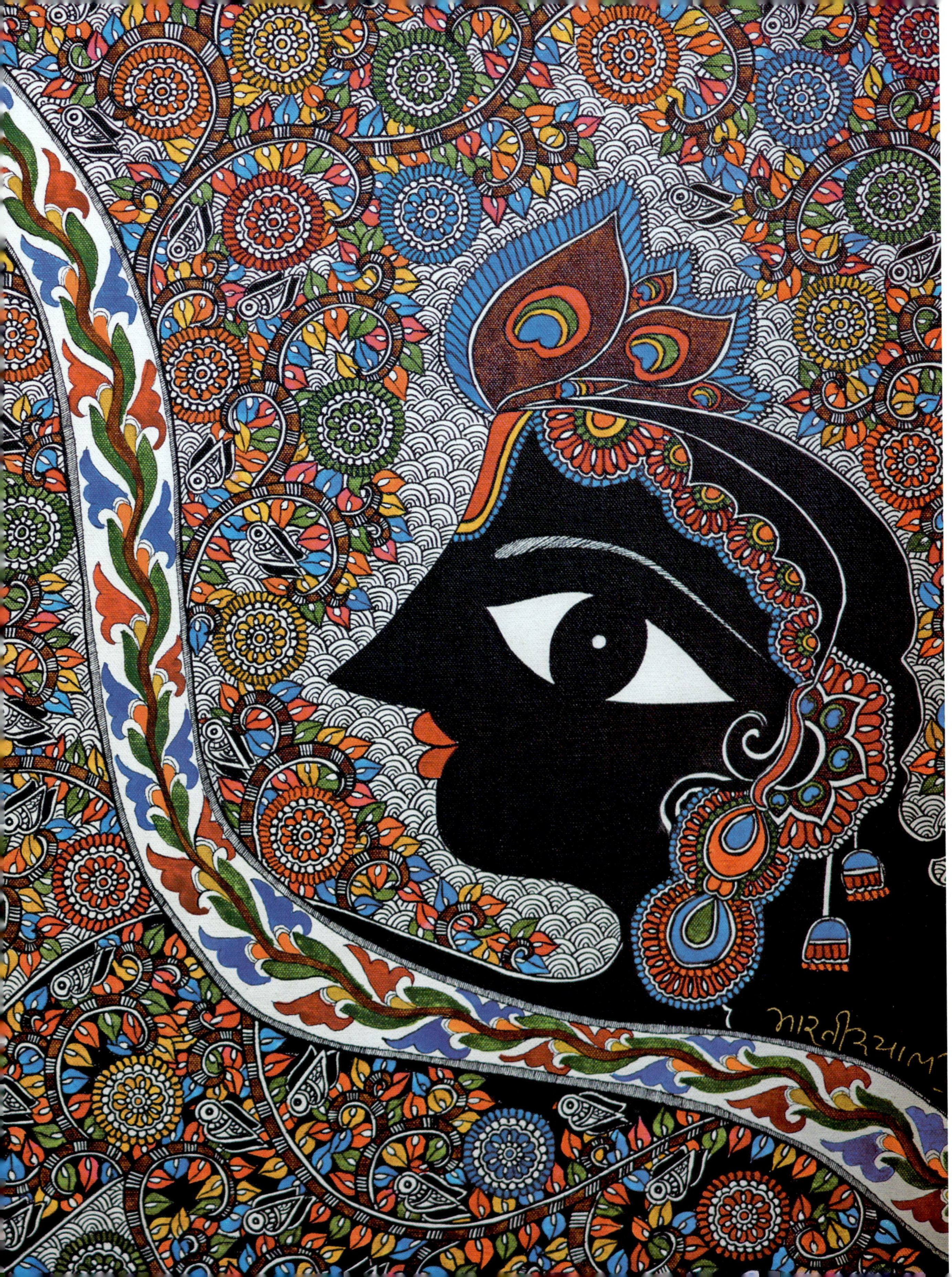

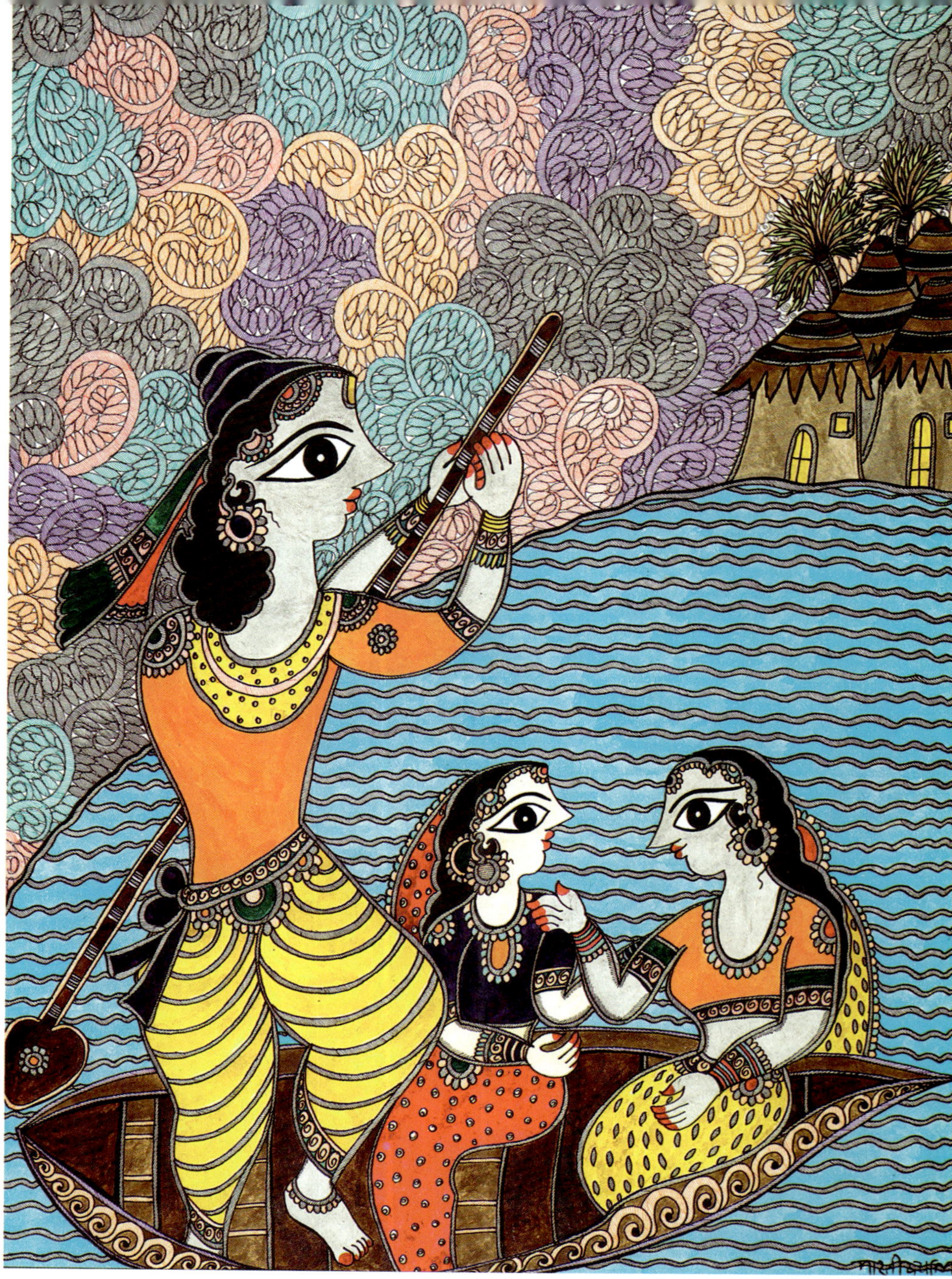

Krishna Rowing a Boat for Gopis
Pigments on Paper, 73 x 53 cm

Gopis Worshipping Radha-Krishna
Pigments on Paper, 110 x 75 cm (p. 41)

Krishna with a Peacock Feather
Acrylic on Canvas, 68 x 92 cm (pp. 38-39)

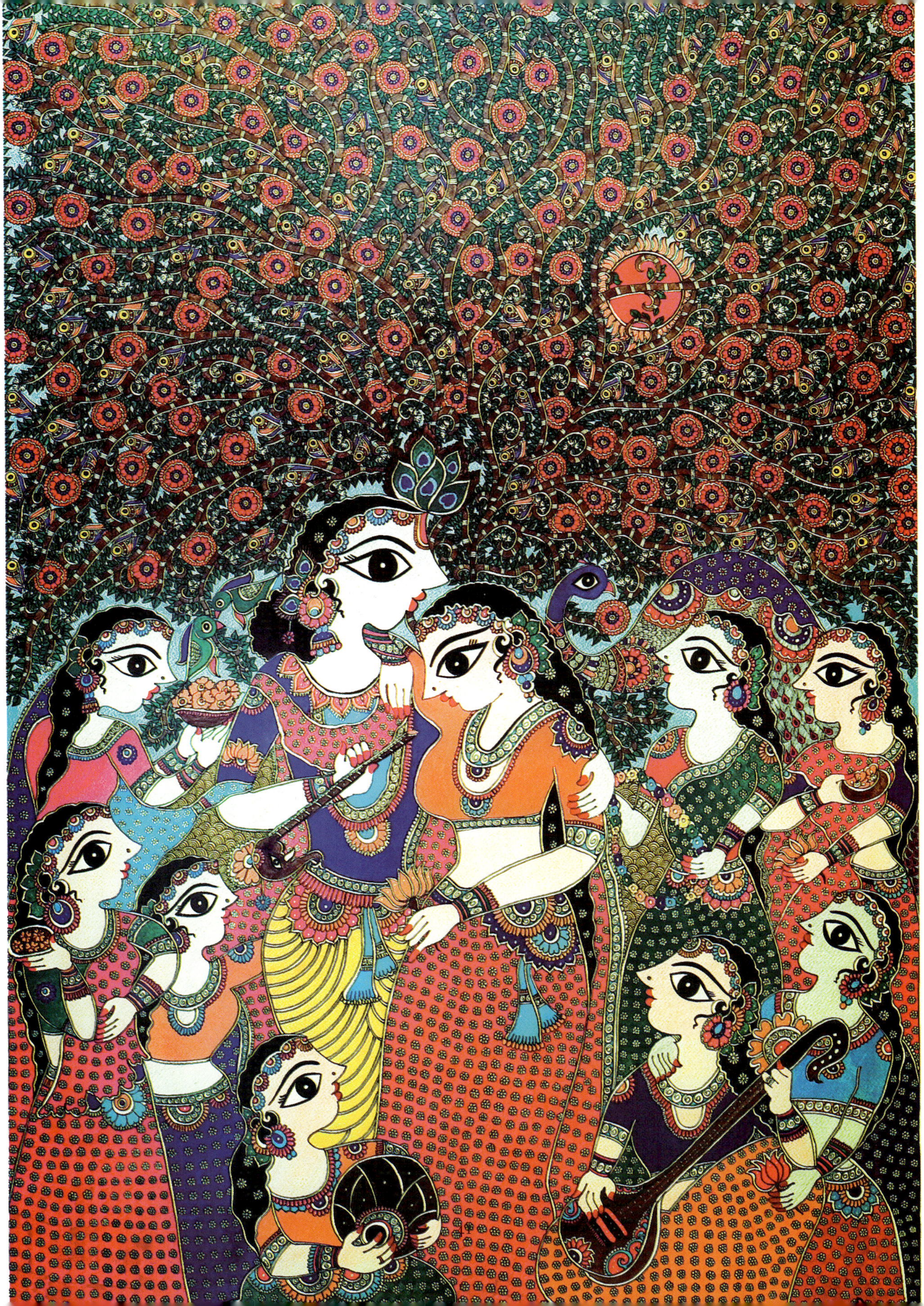

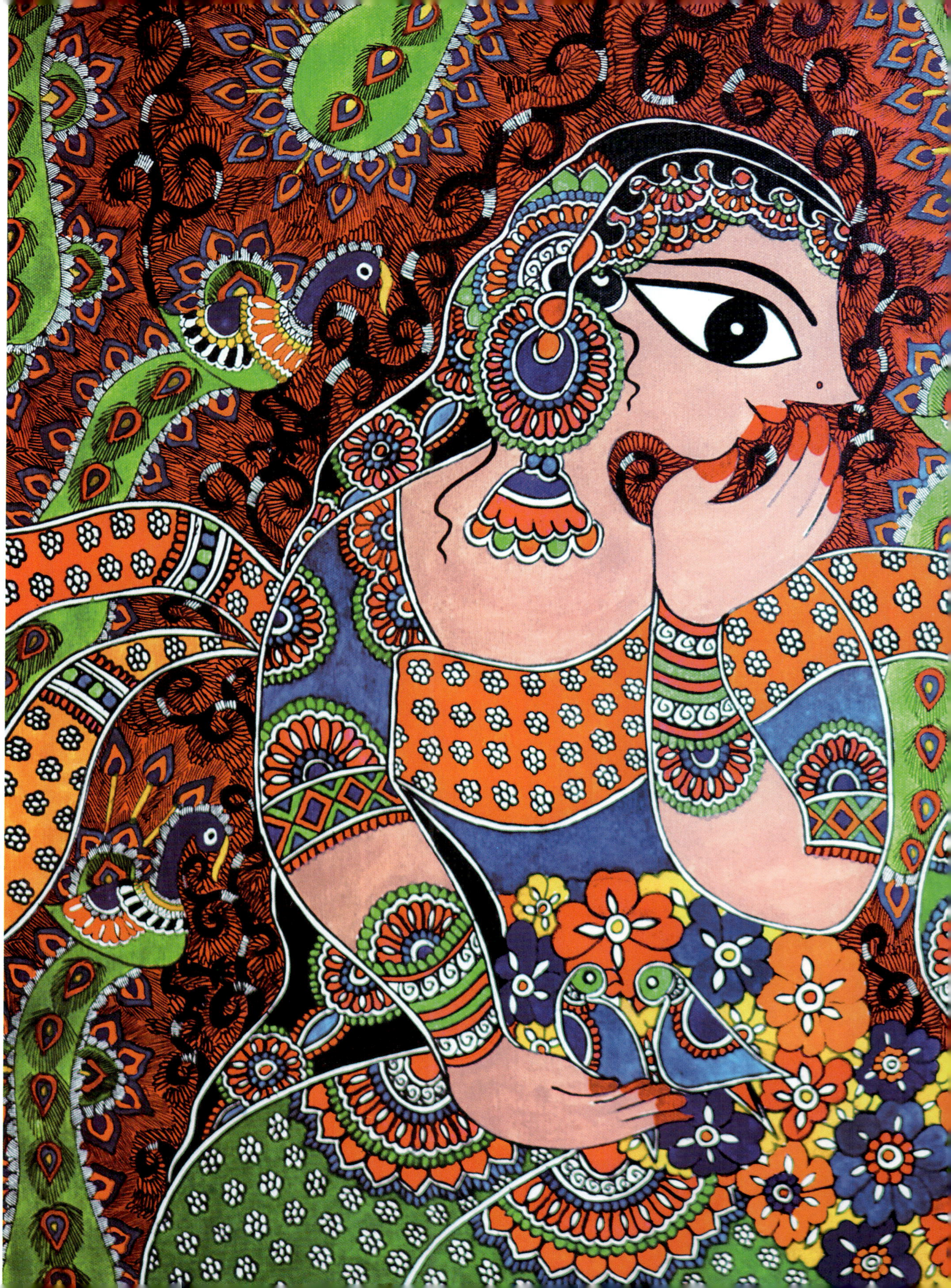

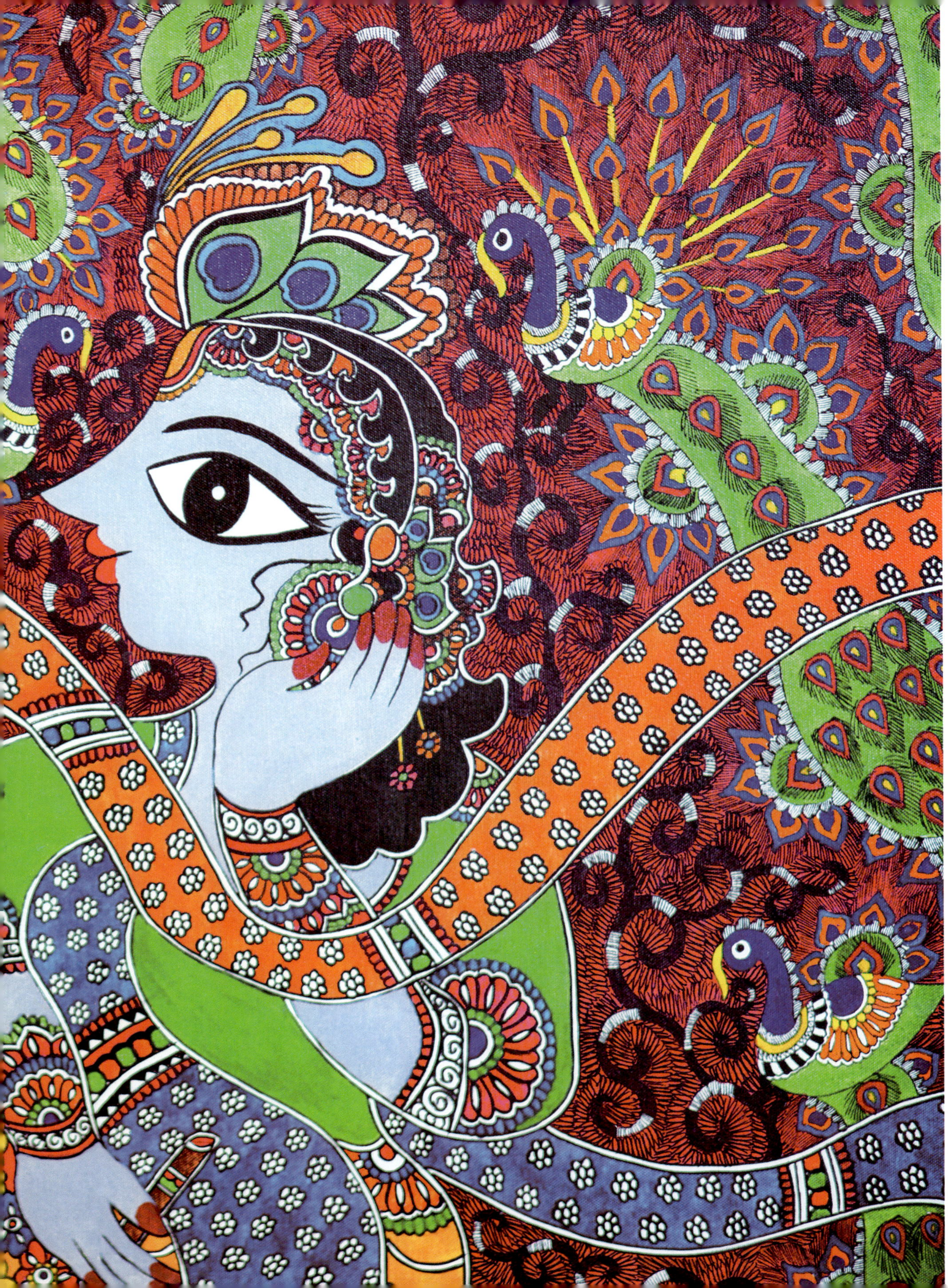

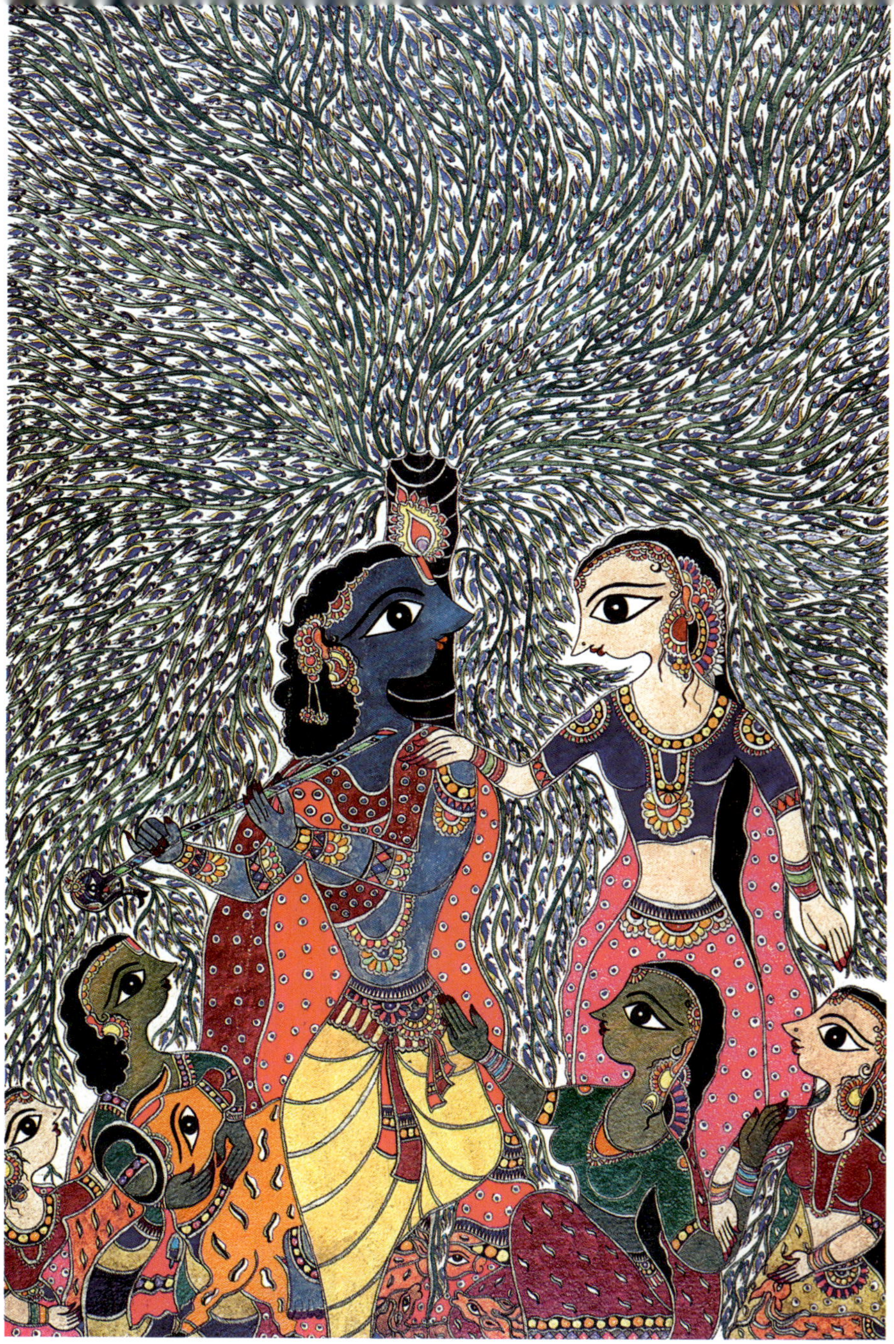

Krishna with Gopis and Cows under a Tree
Pigments on Paper, 97 x 65 cm

Radha-Krishna Watching the Moon
Acrylic on Canvas, 94 x 70 cm (p. 45)

Radha-Krishna with Radha Holding Parrots
Acrylic on Canvas, 81 x 96 cm (pp. 42-43)

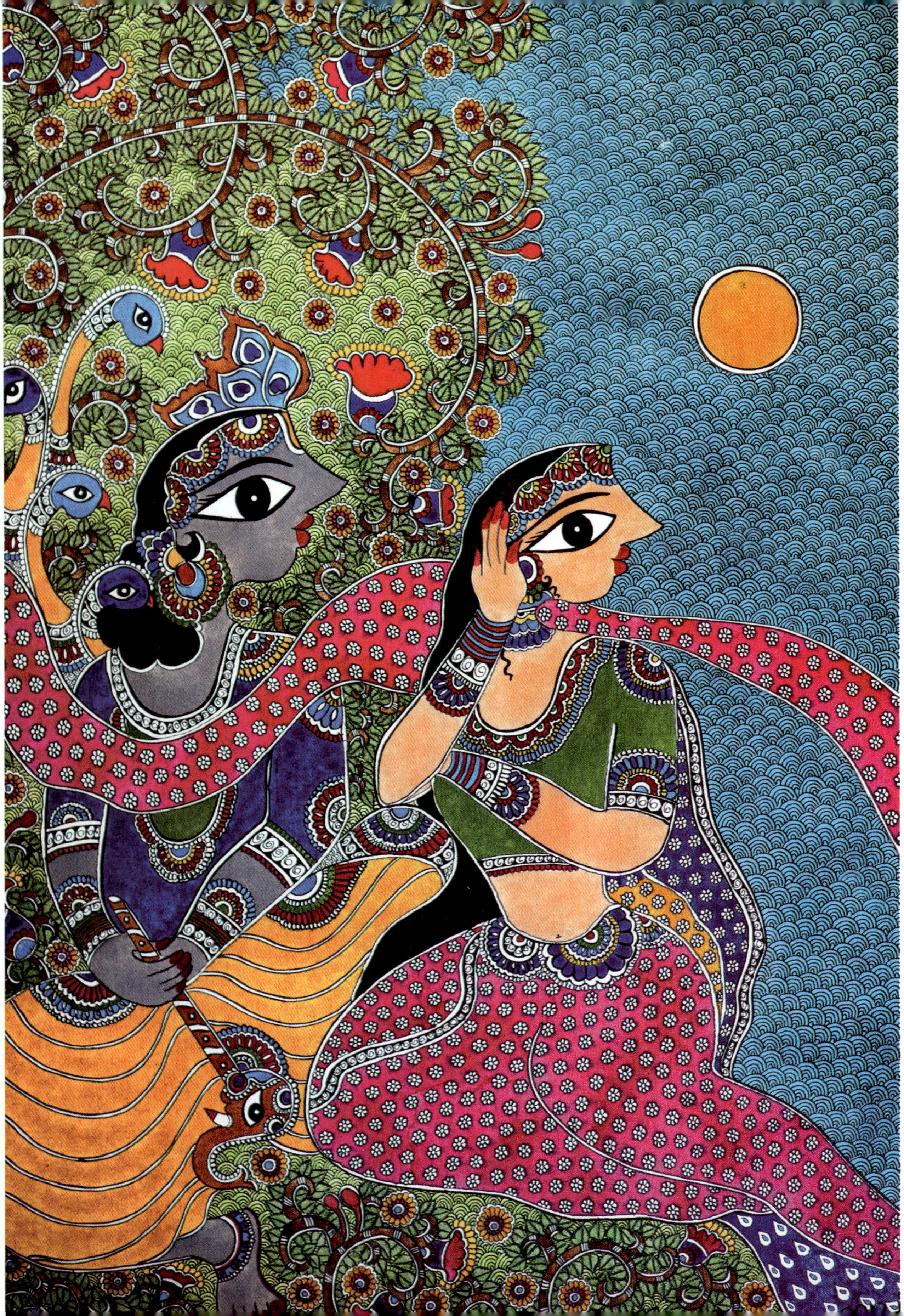

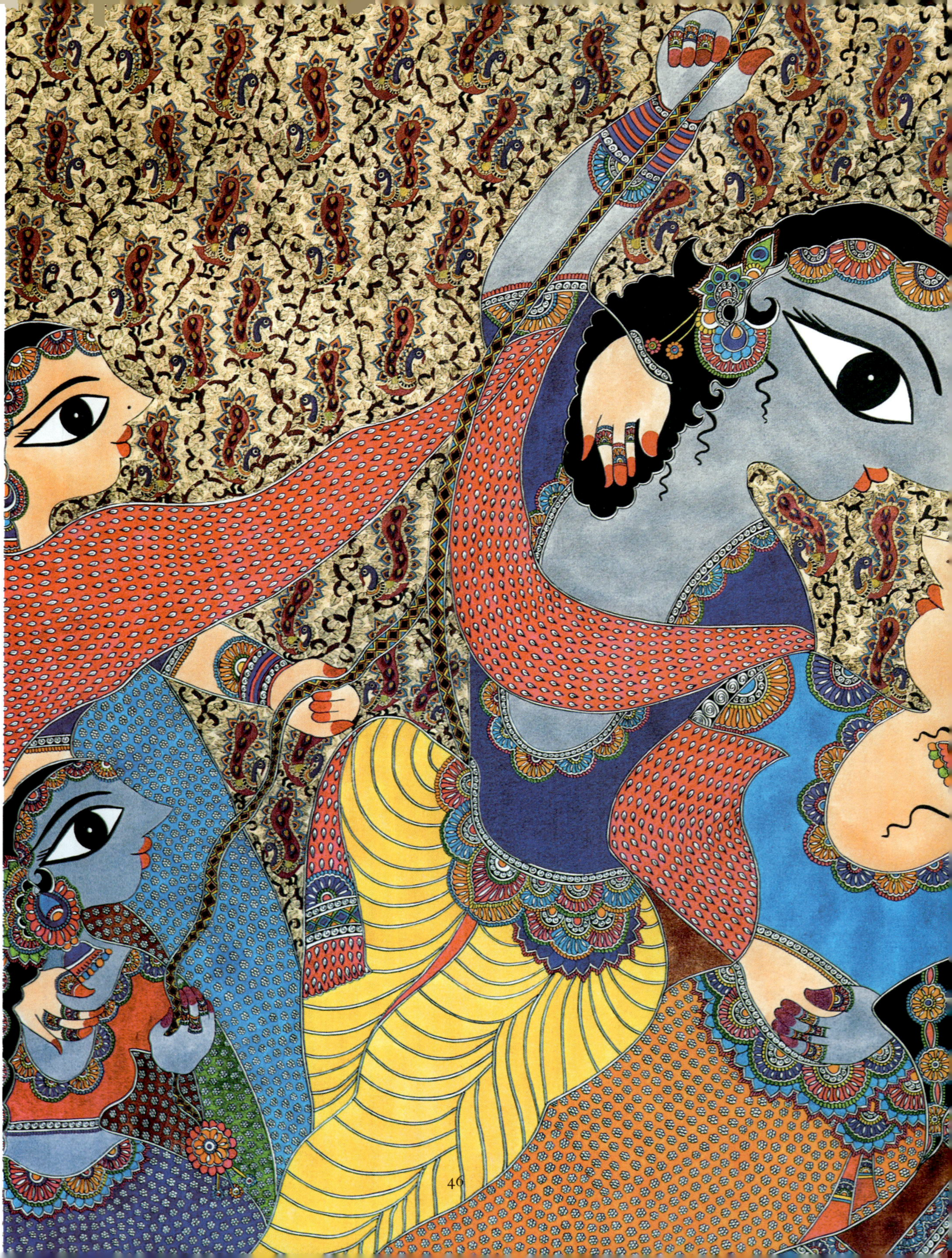

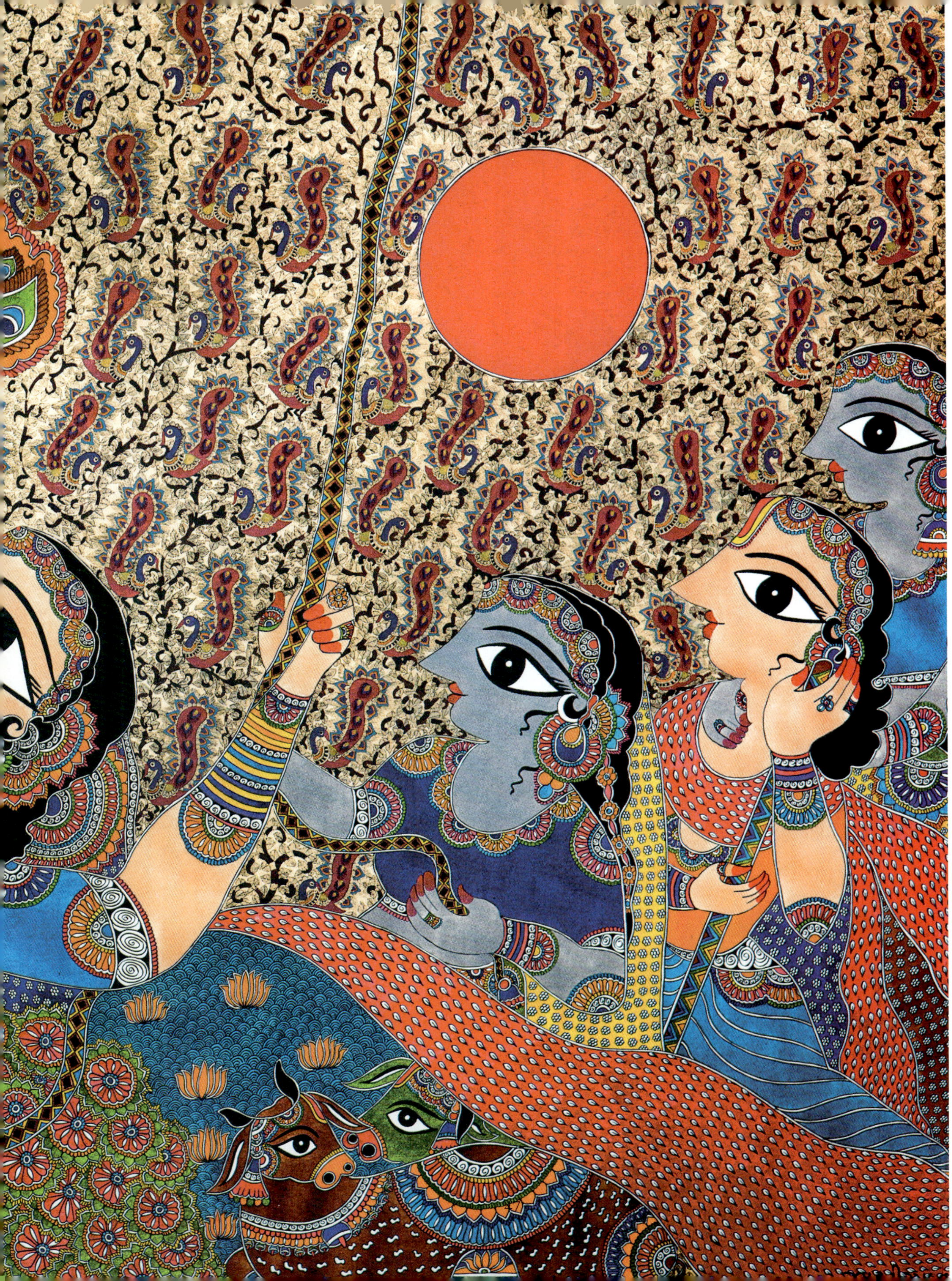

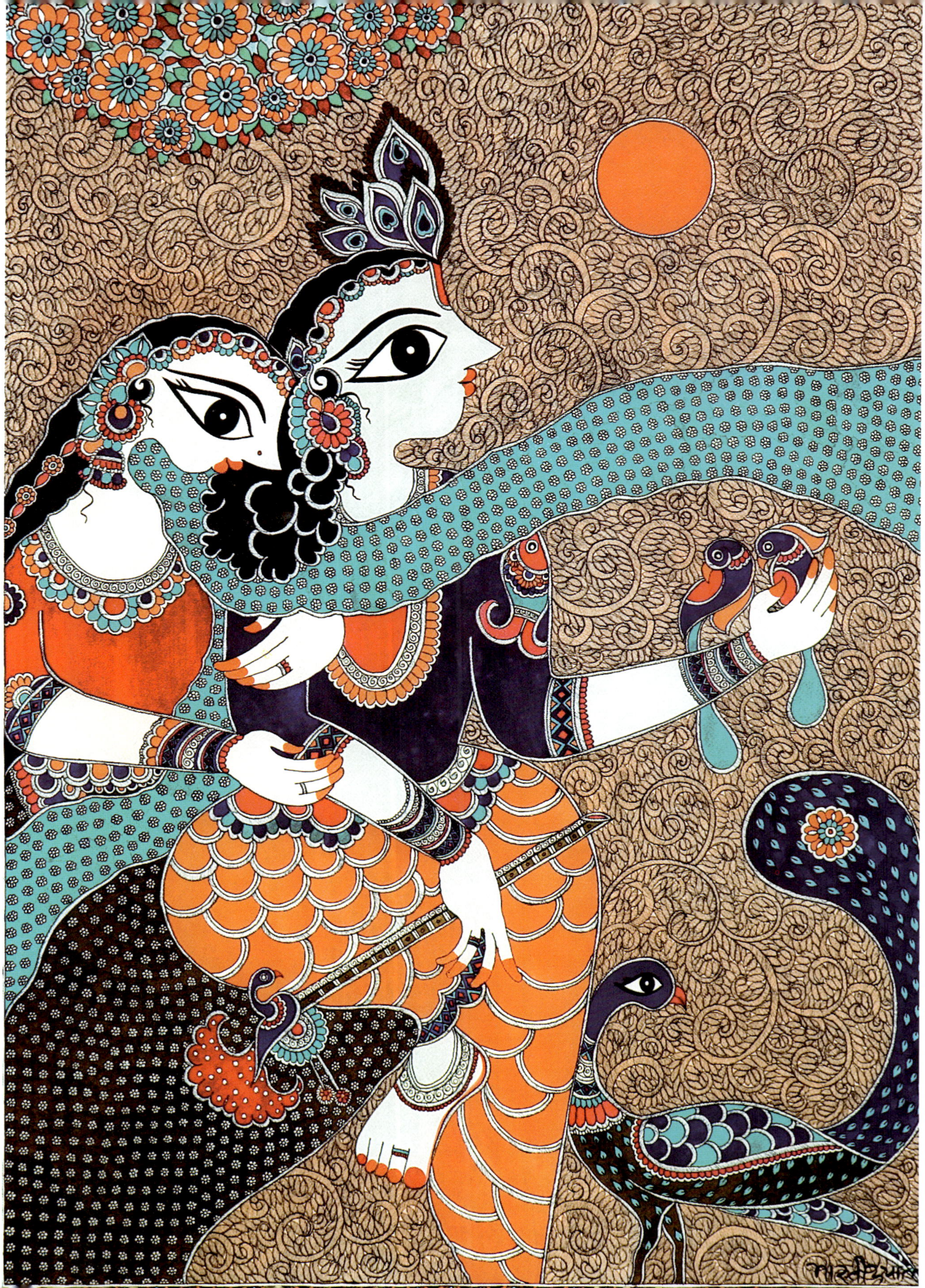

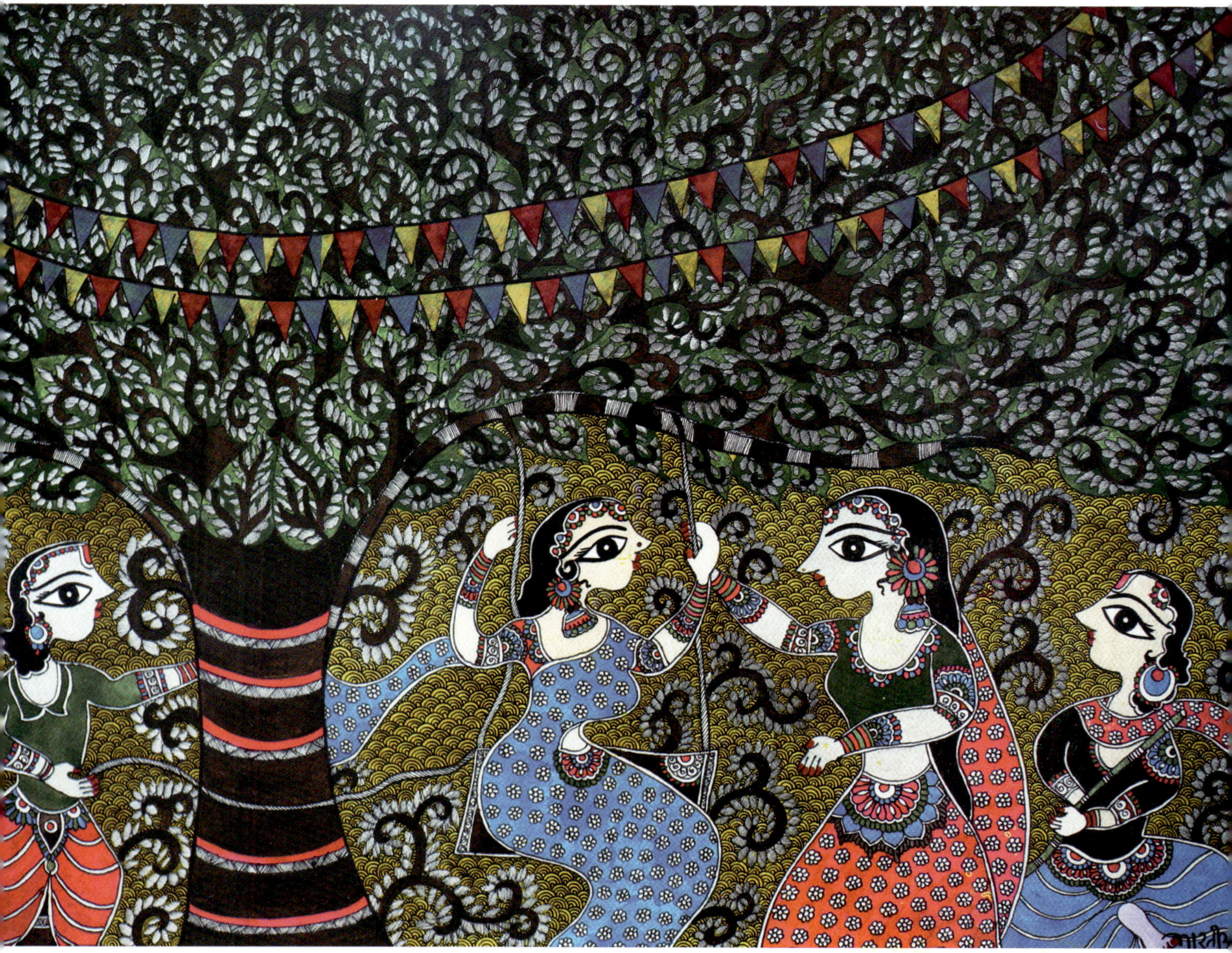

Radha-Krishna Swinging Under a Tree
Pigments on Paper, 55 x 75 cm

Radha-Krishna Holding Parrots
Pigments on Paper, 121 x 99 cm (p. 48)

Radha-Krishna Swinging
Acrylic on Canvas, 180 x 228 cm (pp. 46-47)

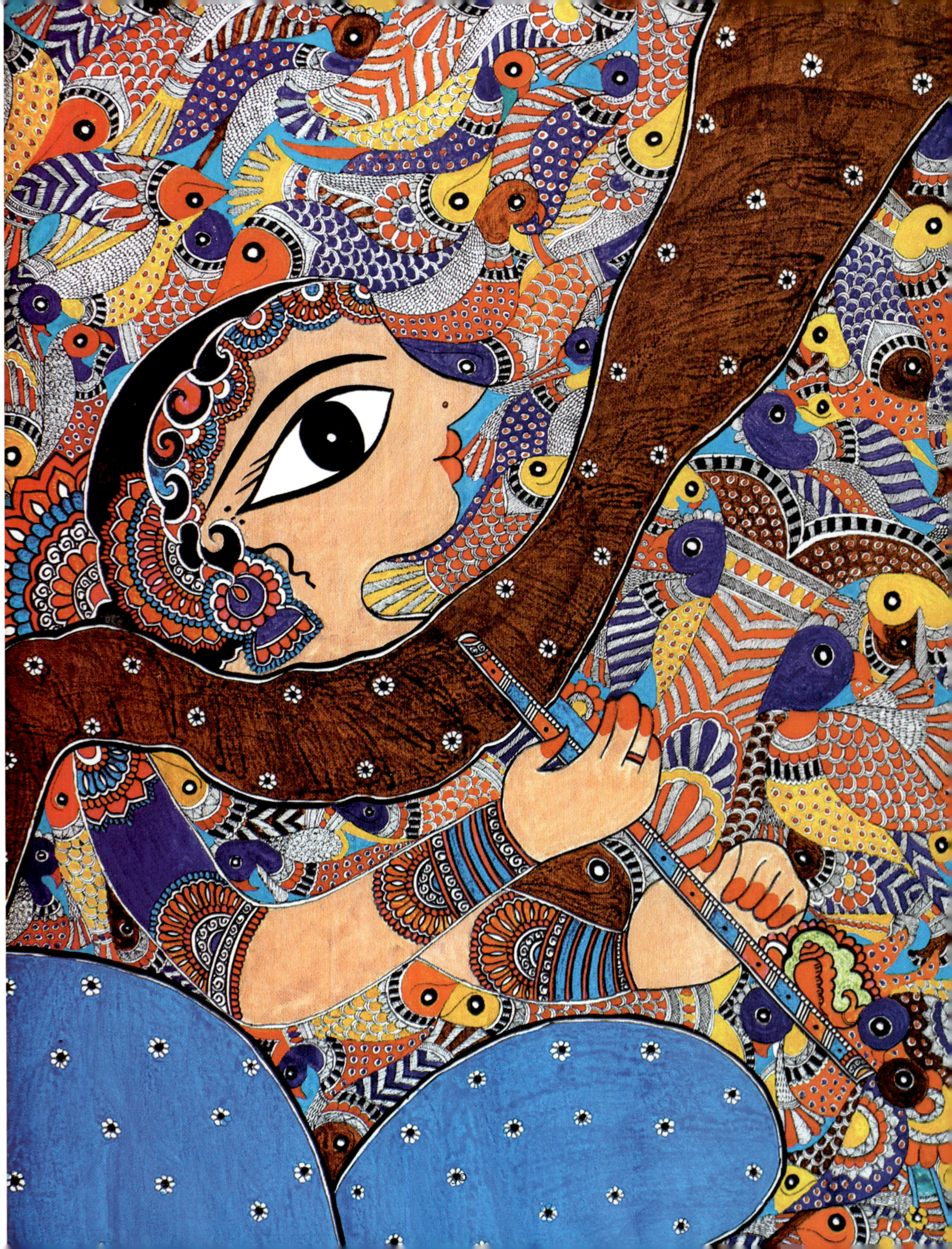

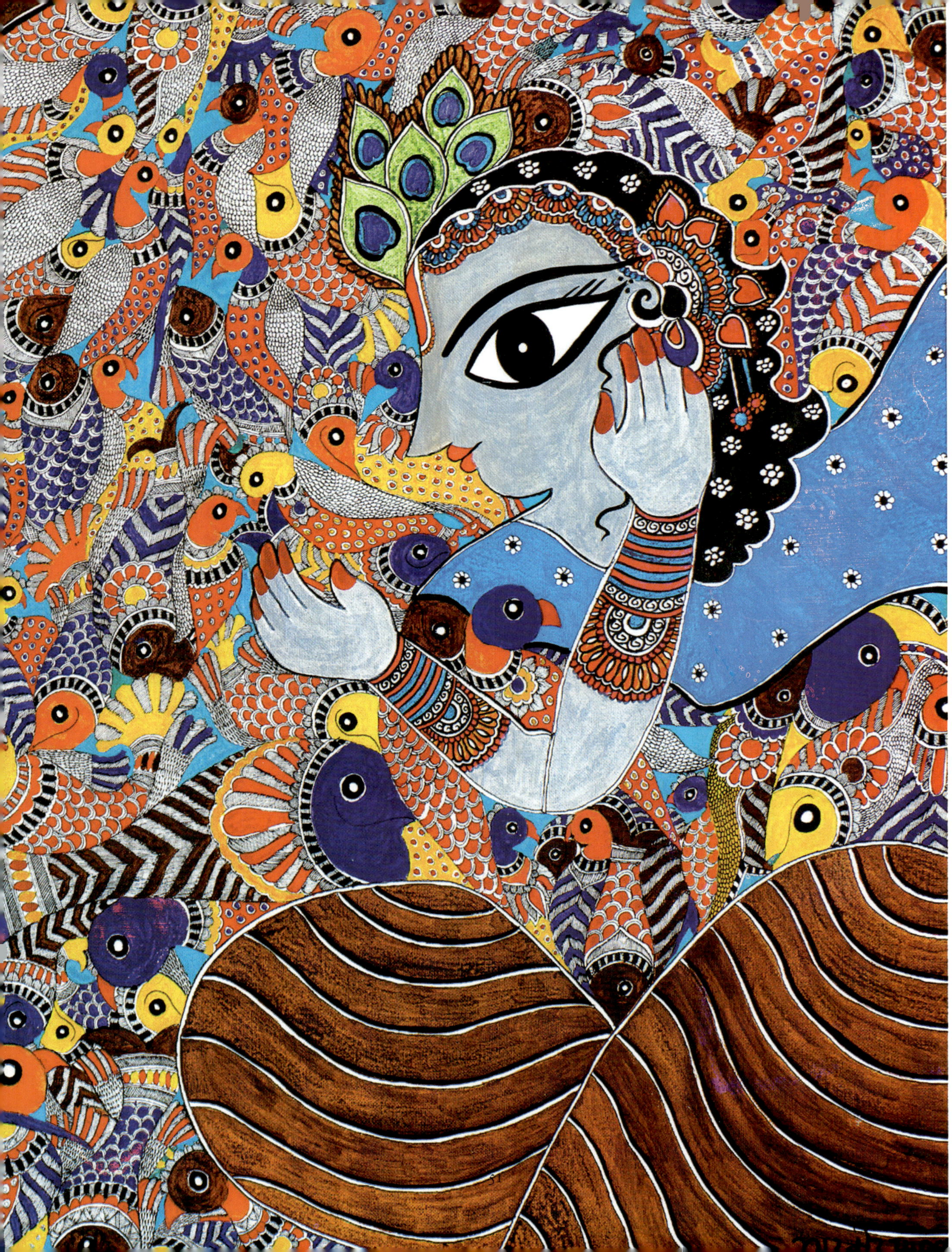

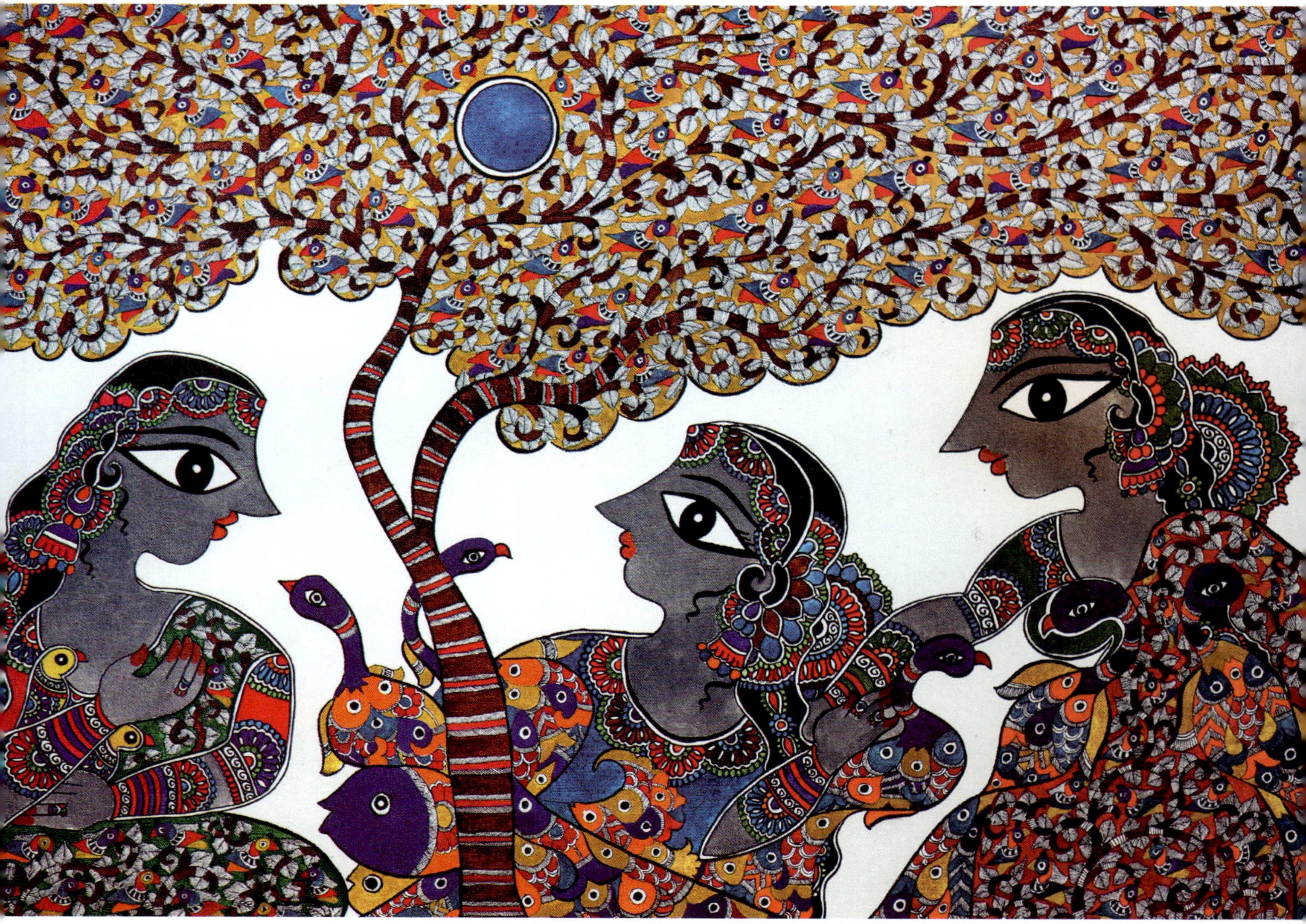

The Gopis Under a Tree
Acrylic on Canvas, 68 x 95 cm

Radha with Krishna's Flute
Pigments on Paper, 121 x 99 cm (p. 53)

Radha-Krishna with Radha holding the Flute
Acrylic on Canvas, 77 x 92 cm (50-51)

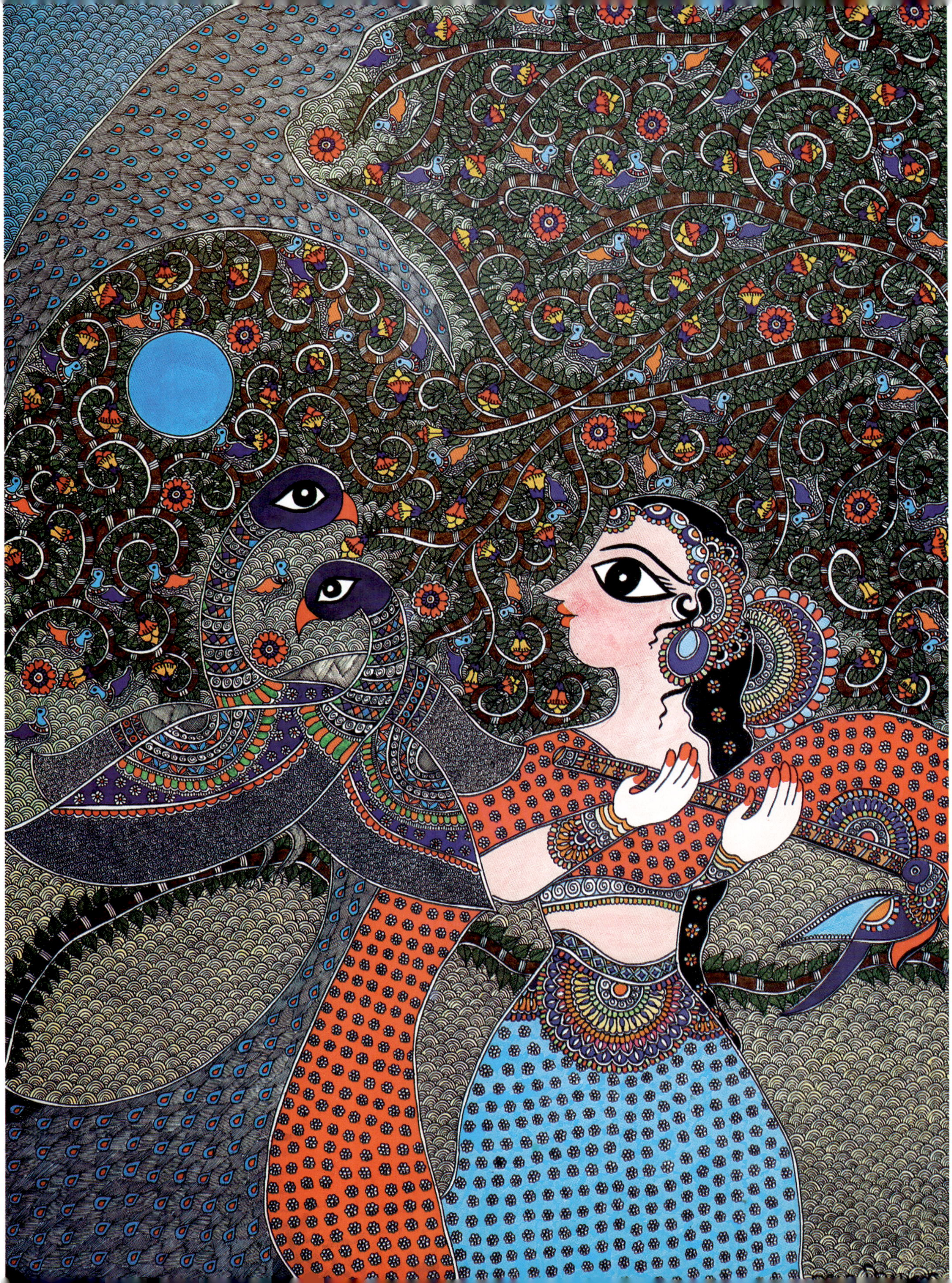

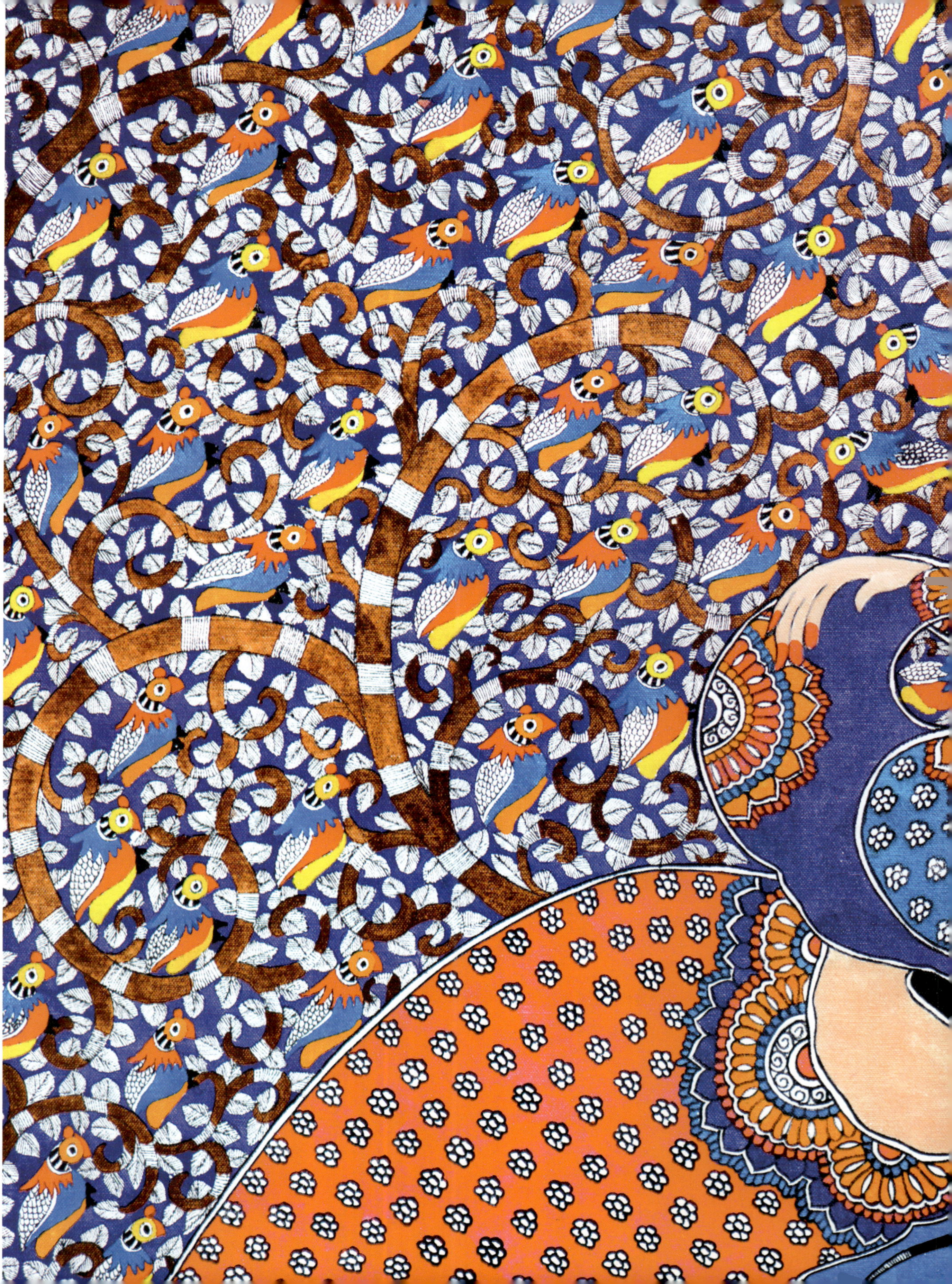

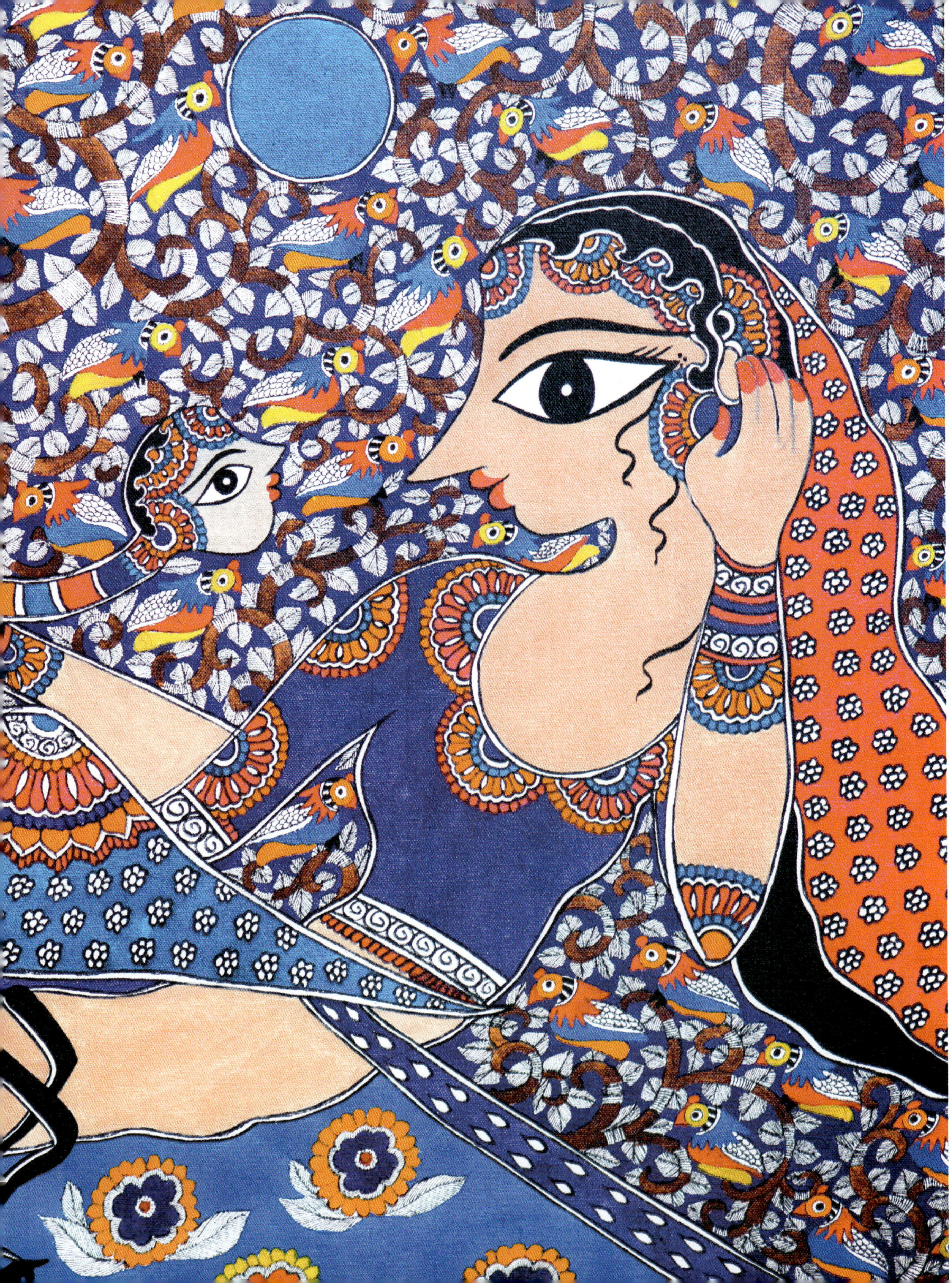

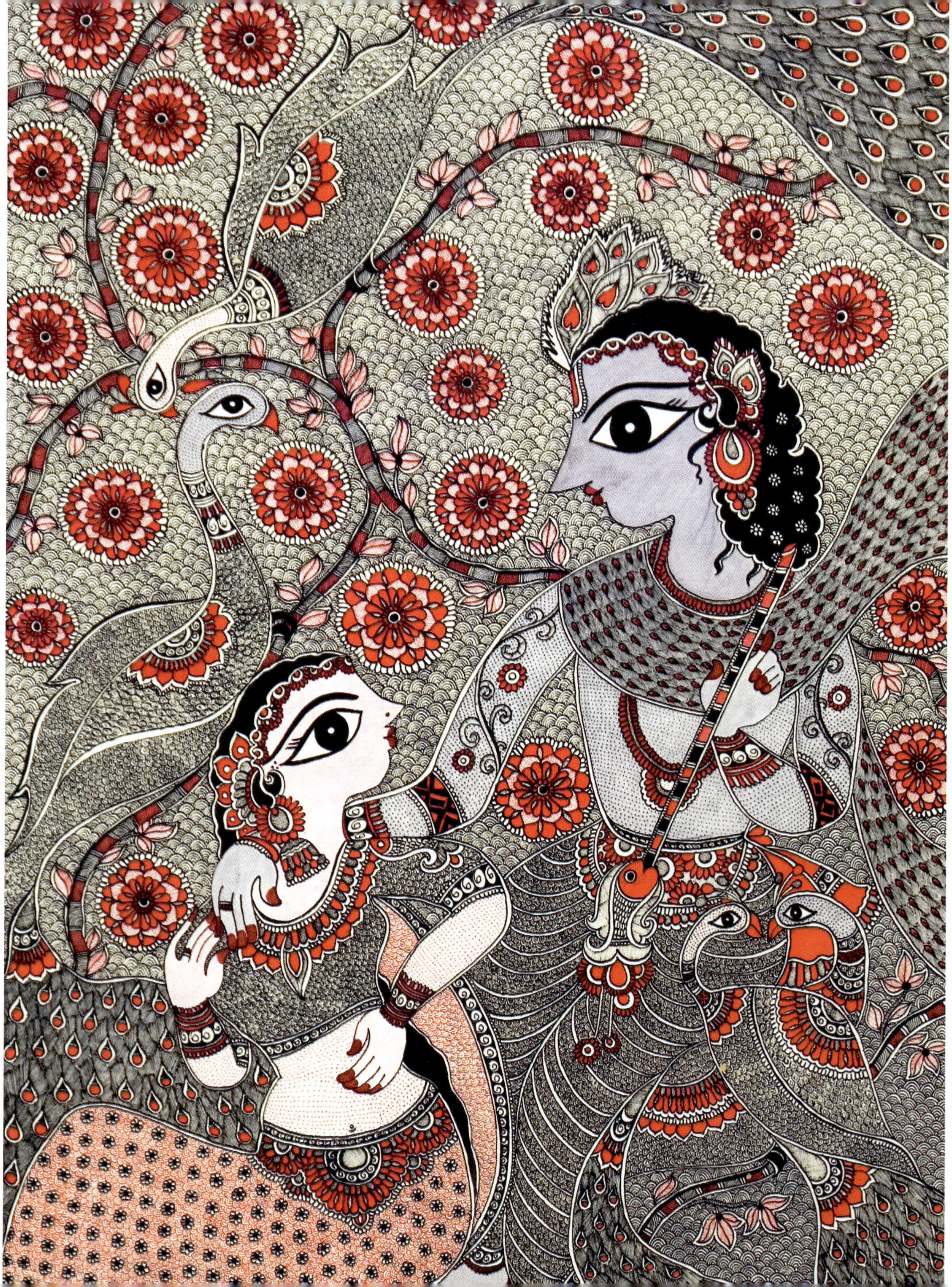

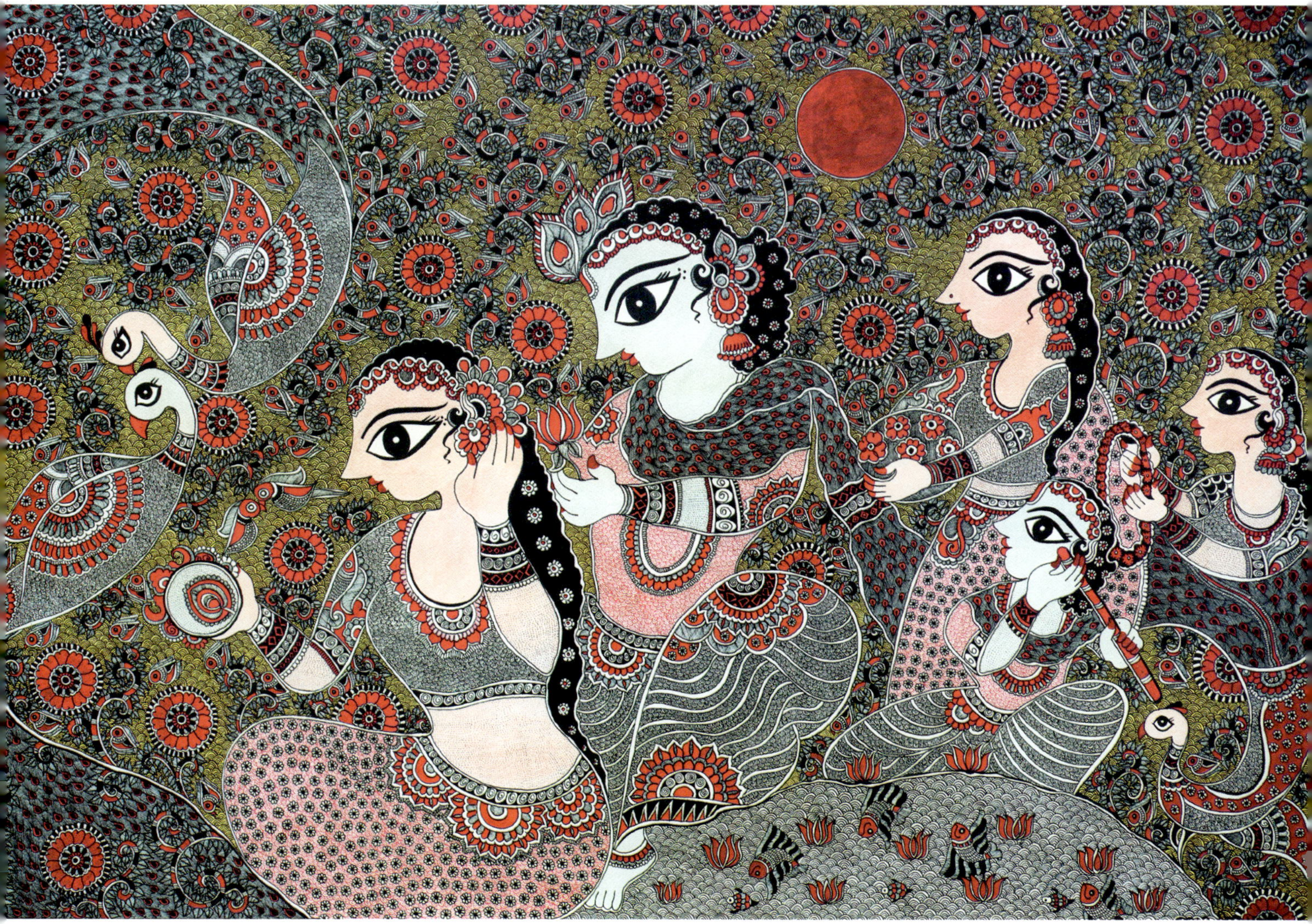

Krishna Giving Radharani a Flower
Pigments on Paper, 72 x 105 cm

Krishna with His Hand Around Radharani
Pigments on Paper, 75 x 55 cm (p. 56)

Radharani
Acrylic on Canvas, 71 x 96 cm (pp. 54-55)

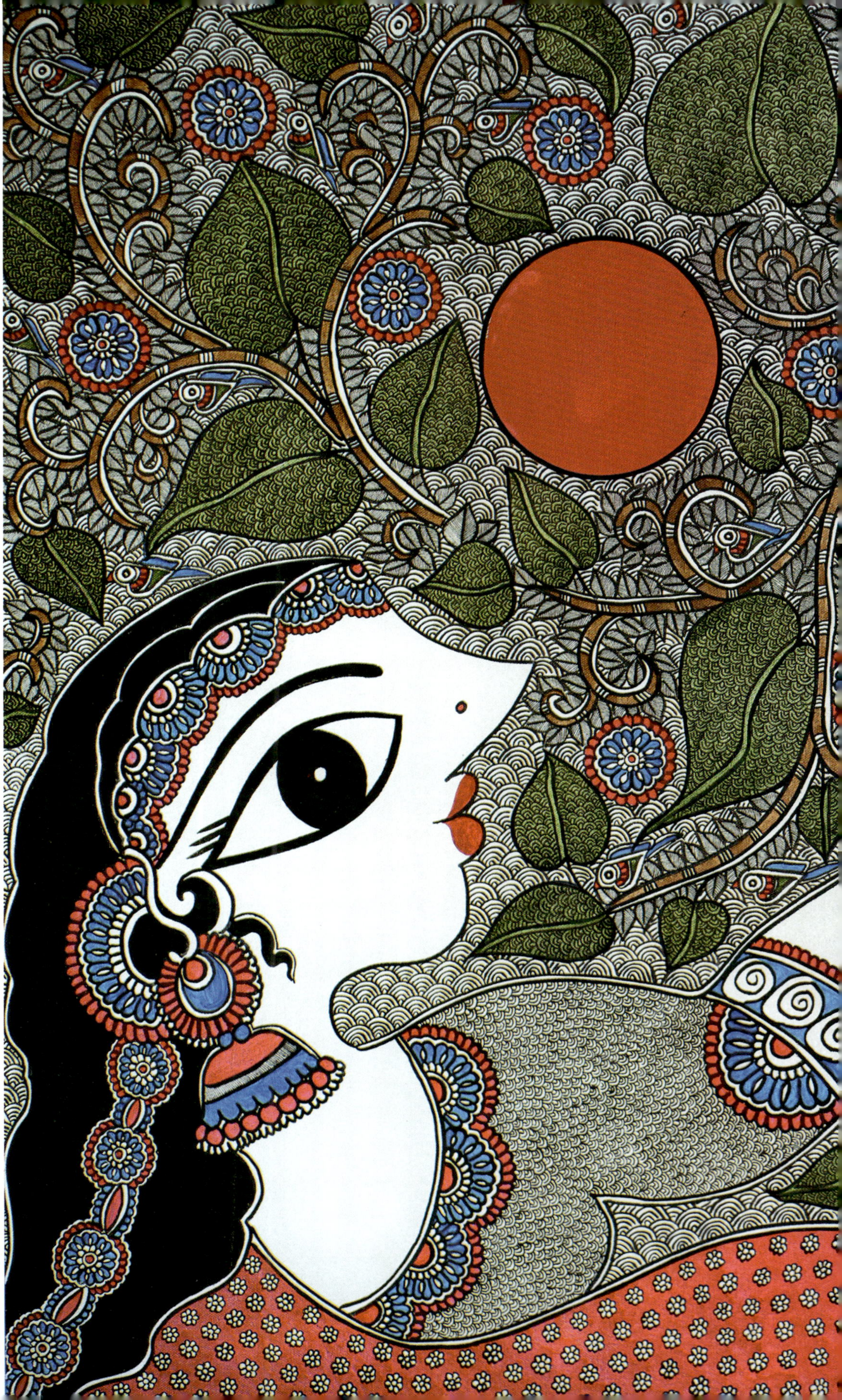

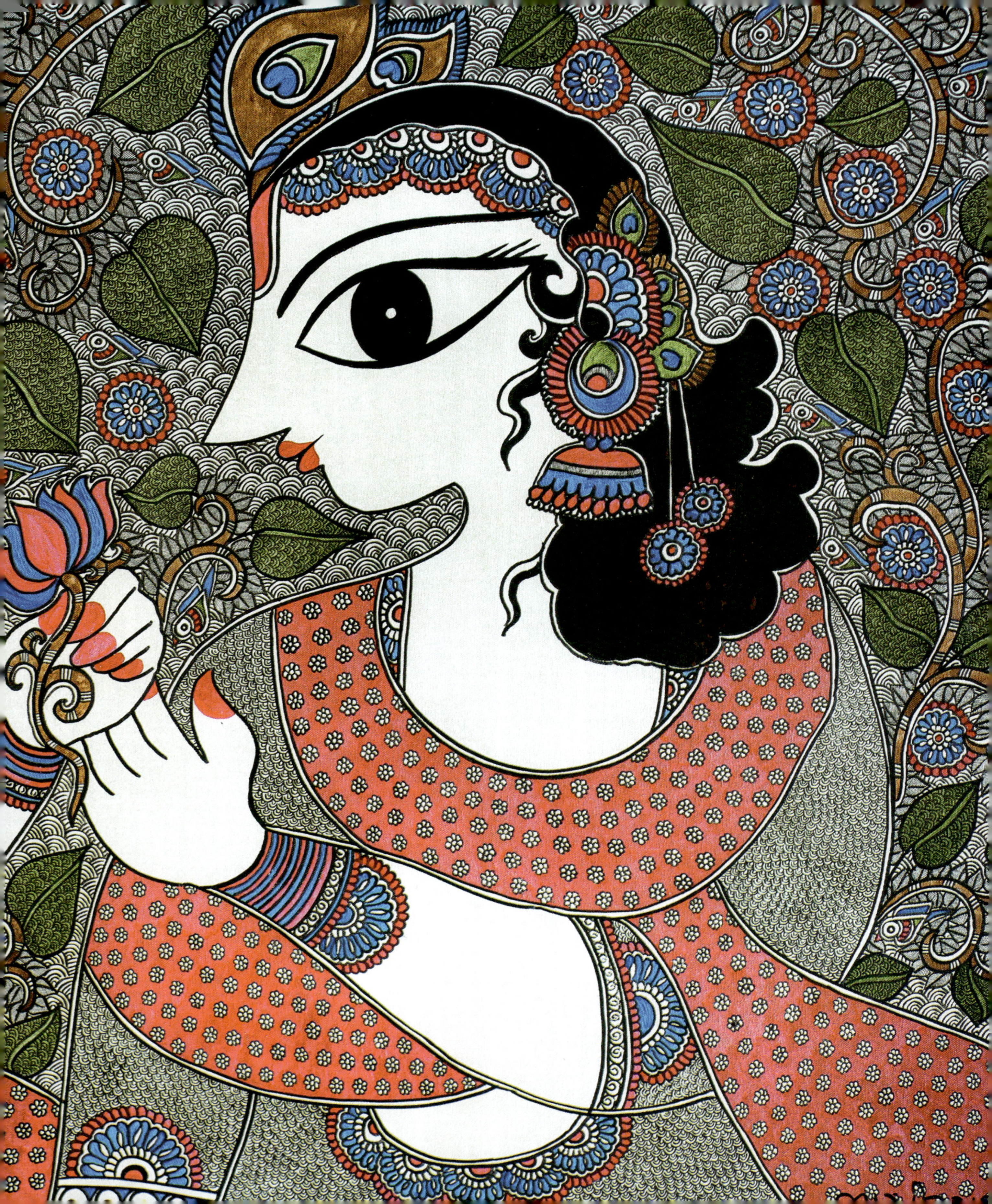

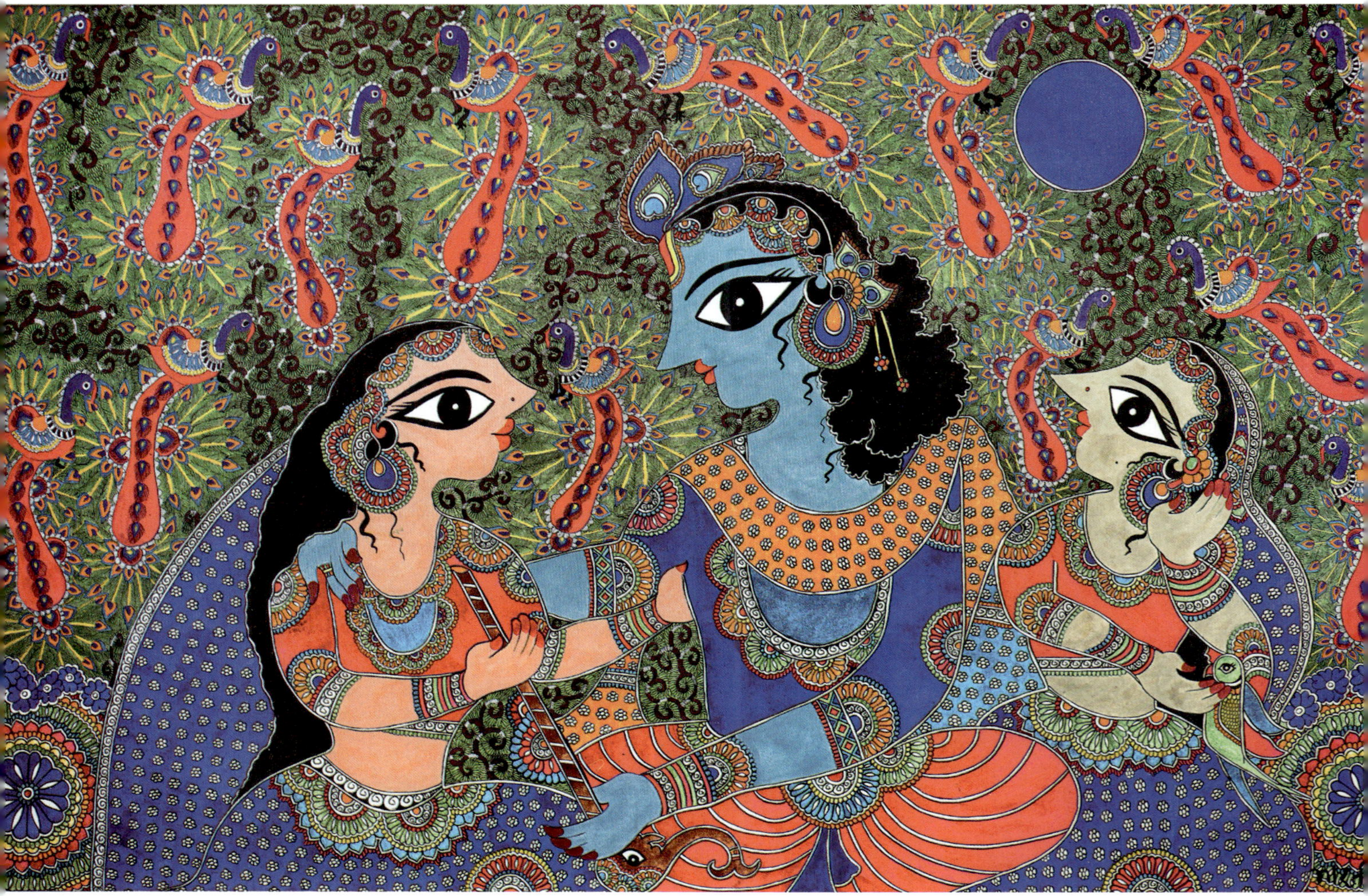

Radha-Krishna Surrounded by Peacocks
Acrylic on Canvas, 95 x 152 cm

Radha-Krishna Dancing
Pigments on Paper, 108 x 73 cm (p. 61)

Radharani Giving Krishna a Flower
Acrylic on Canvas, 85 x 125 cm (pp. 58-59)

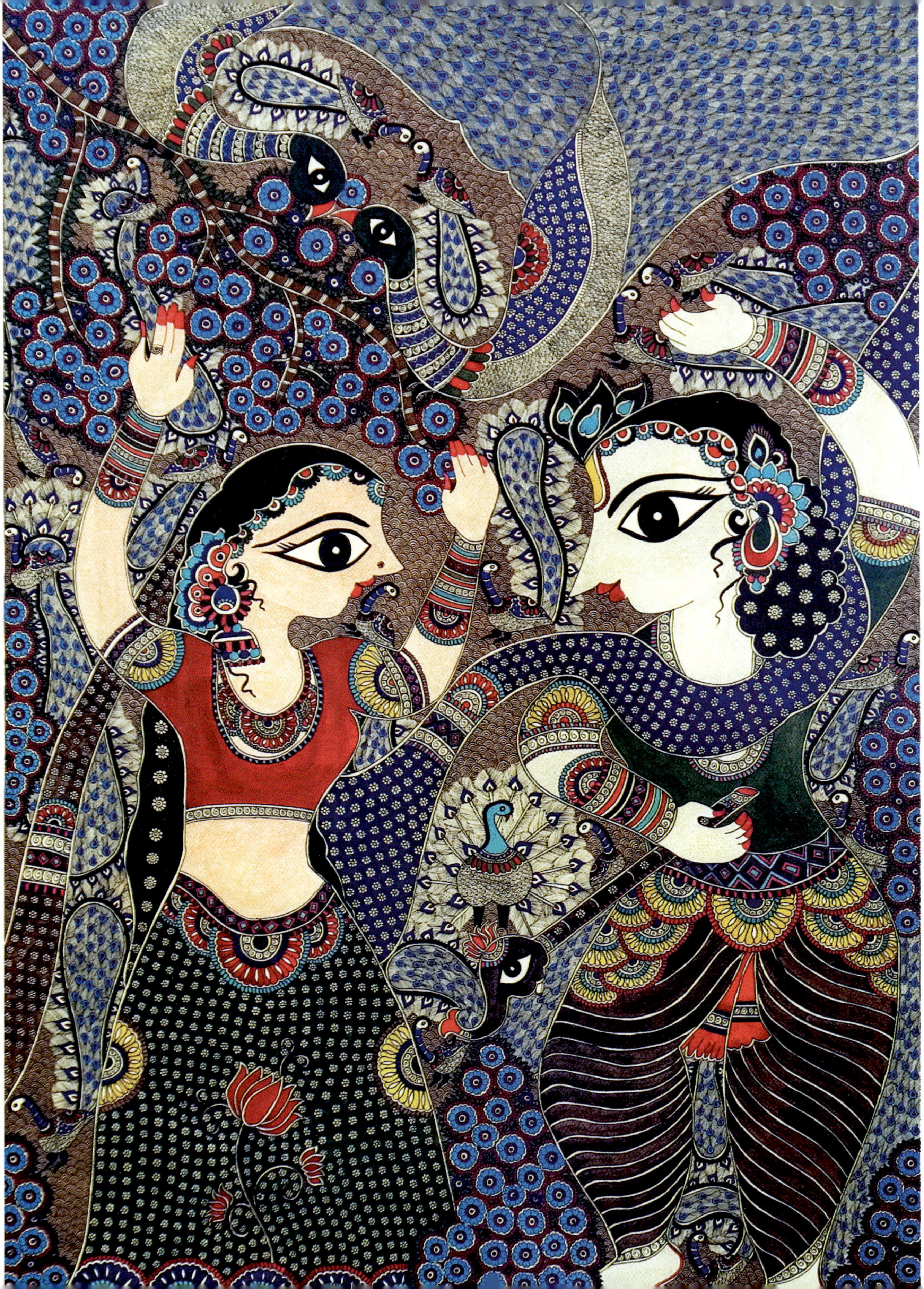

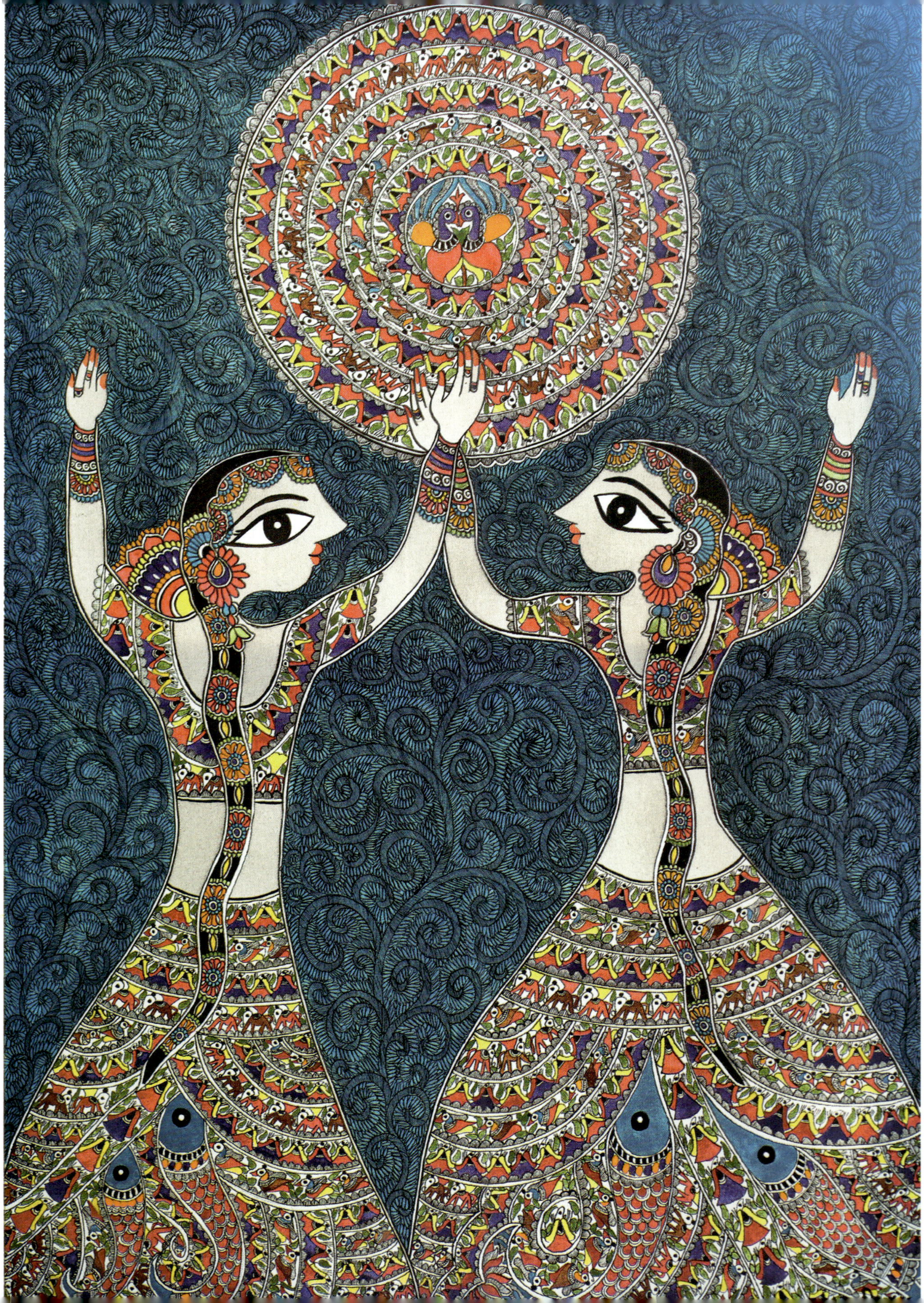

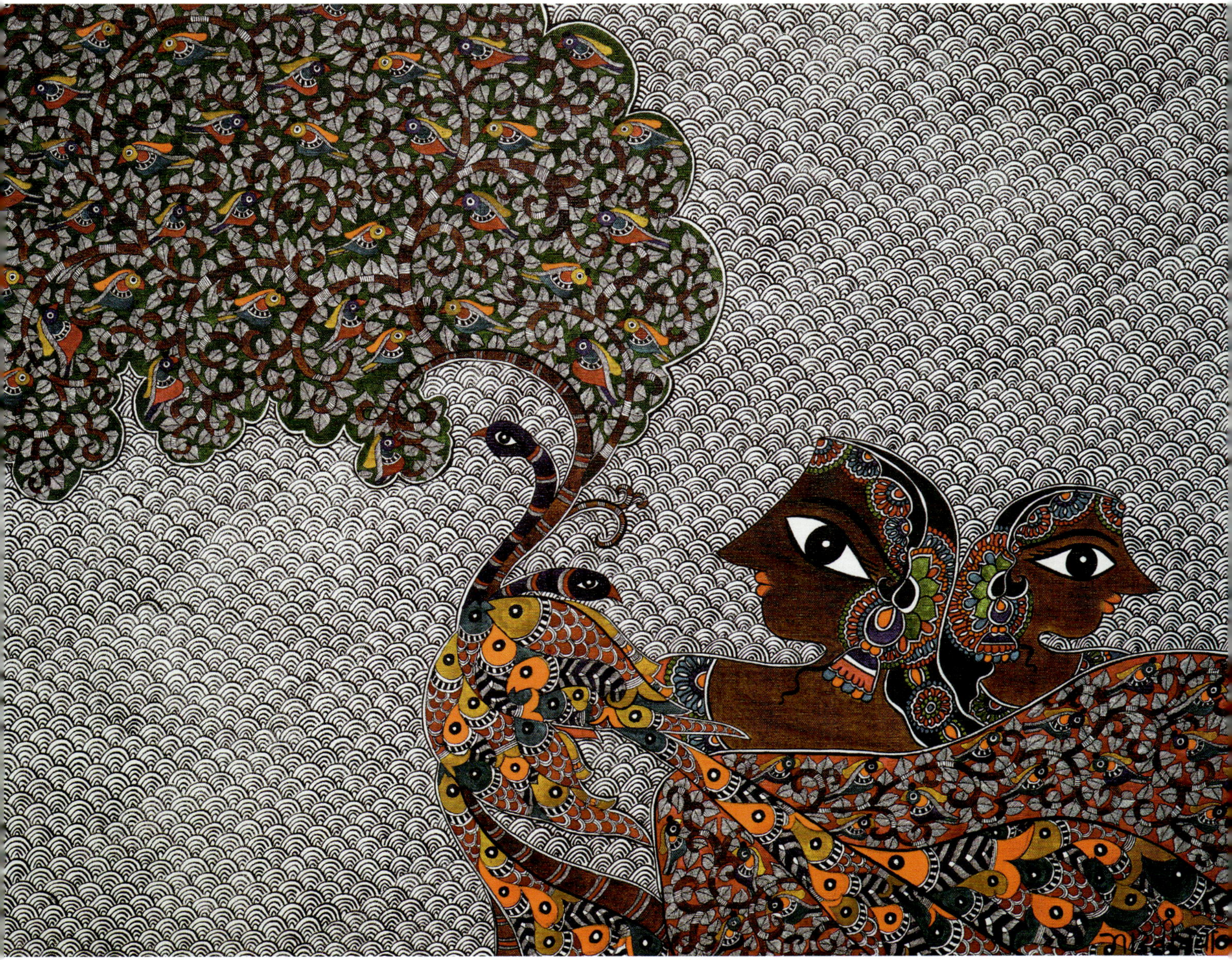

Radha-Krishna Under a Tree
Acrylic on Canvas, 69 x 92 cm

Gopis Dancing
Acrylic on Canvas, 98 x 68 cm (p. 62)

Gopis in the Forest
Acrylic on Canvas, 90 x 139 cm (pp. 64-65)

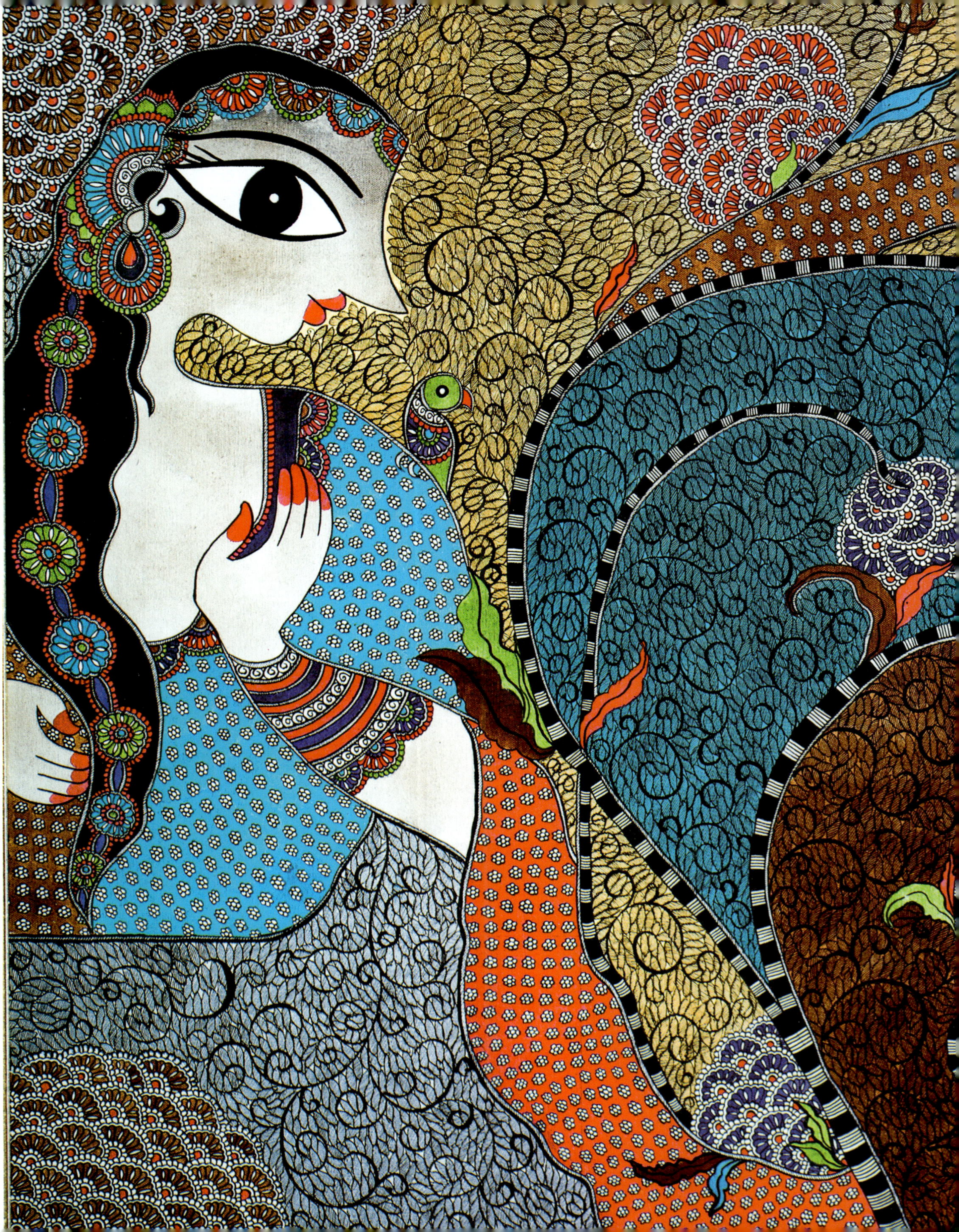

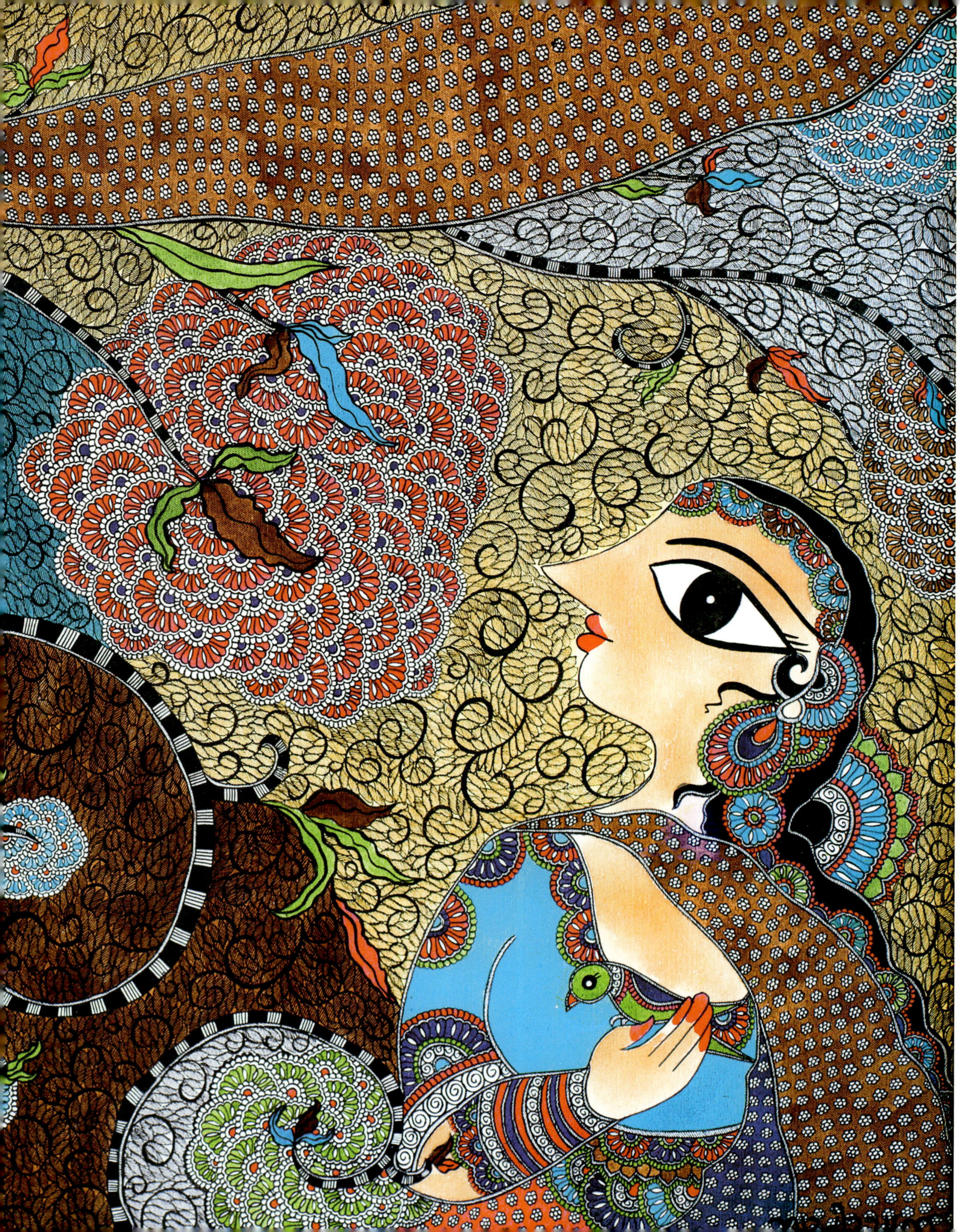

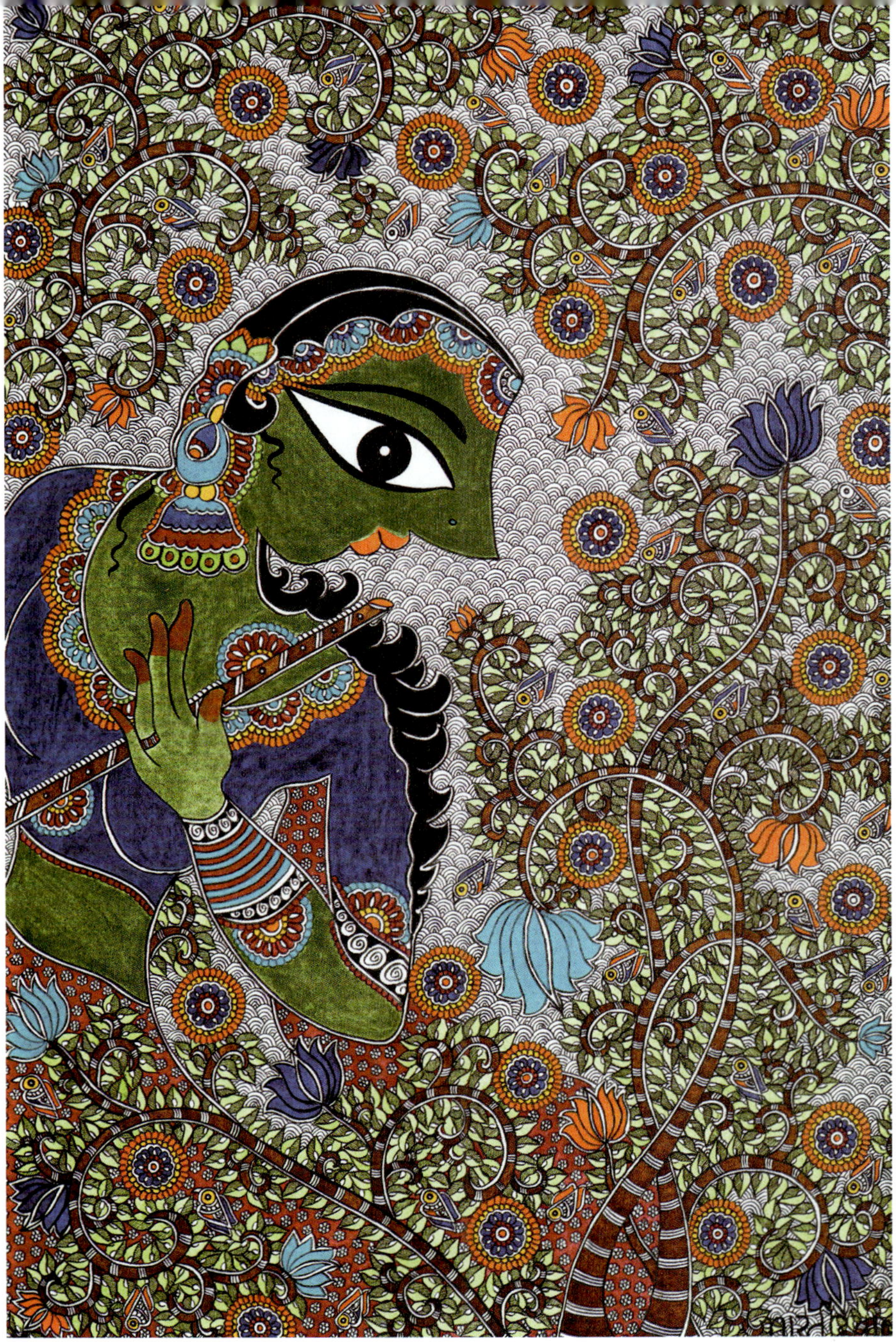

Radharani with Krishna's Flute
Pigments on Paper, 92 x 61 cm

Krishna with Gopis Playing Flute
Acrylic on Canvas, 90 x 60 cm (p. 67)

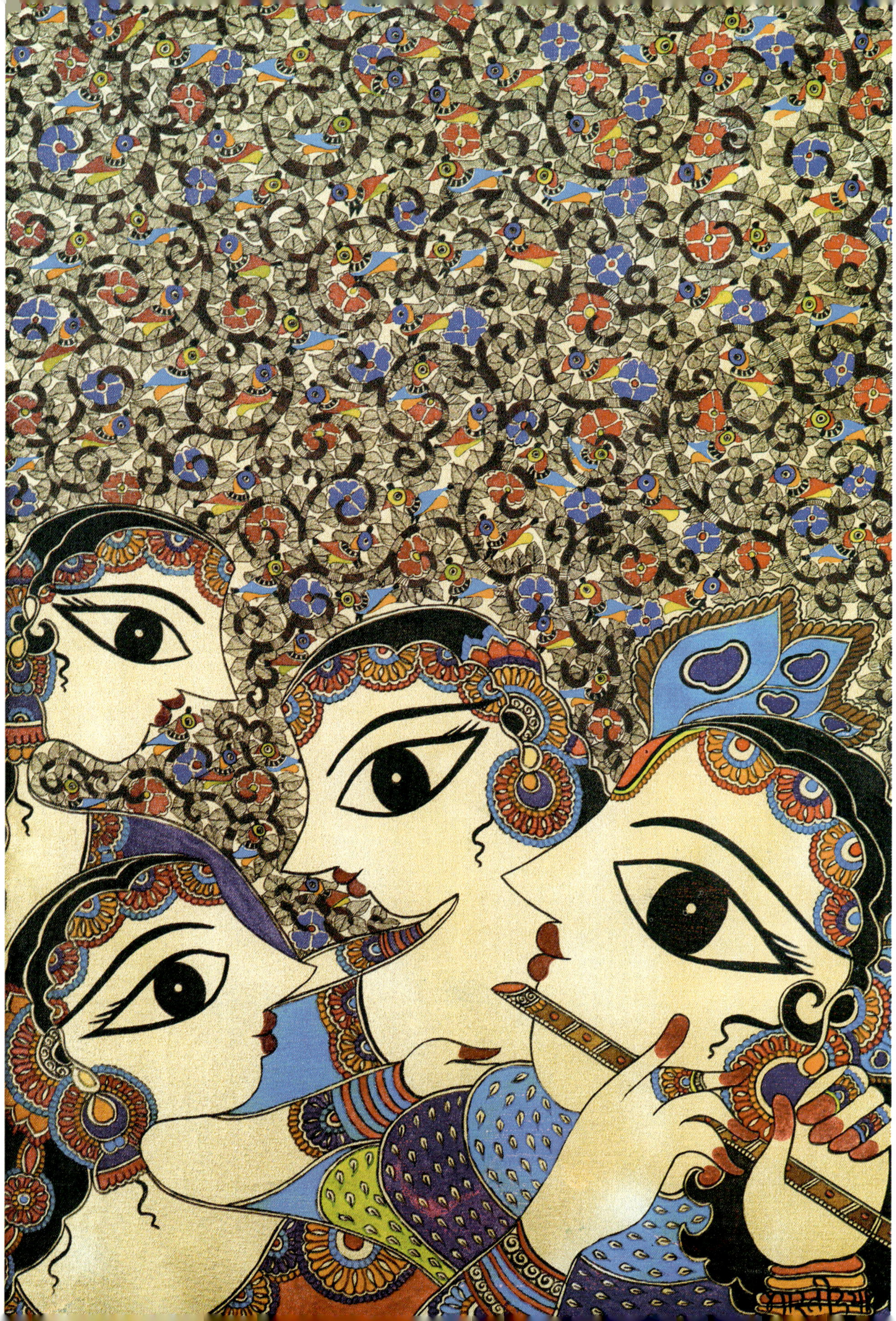

SHIVA

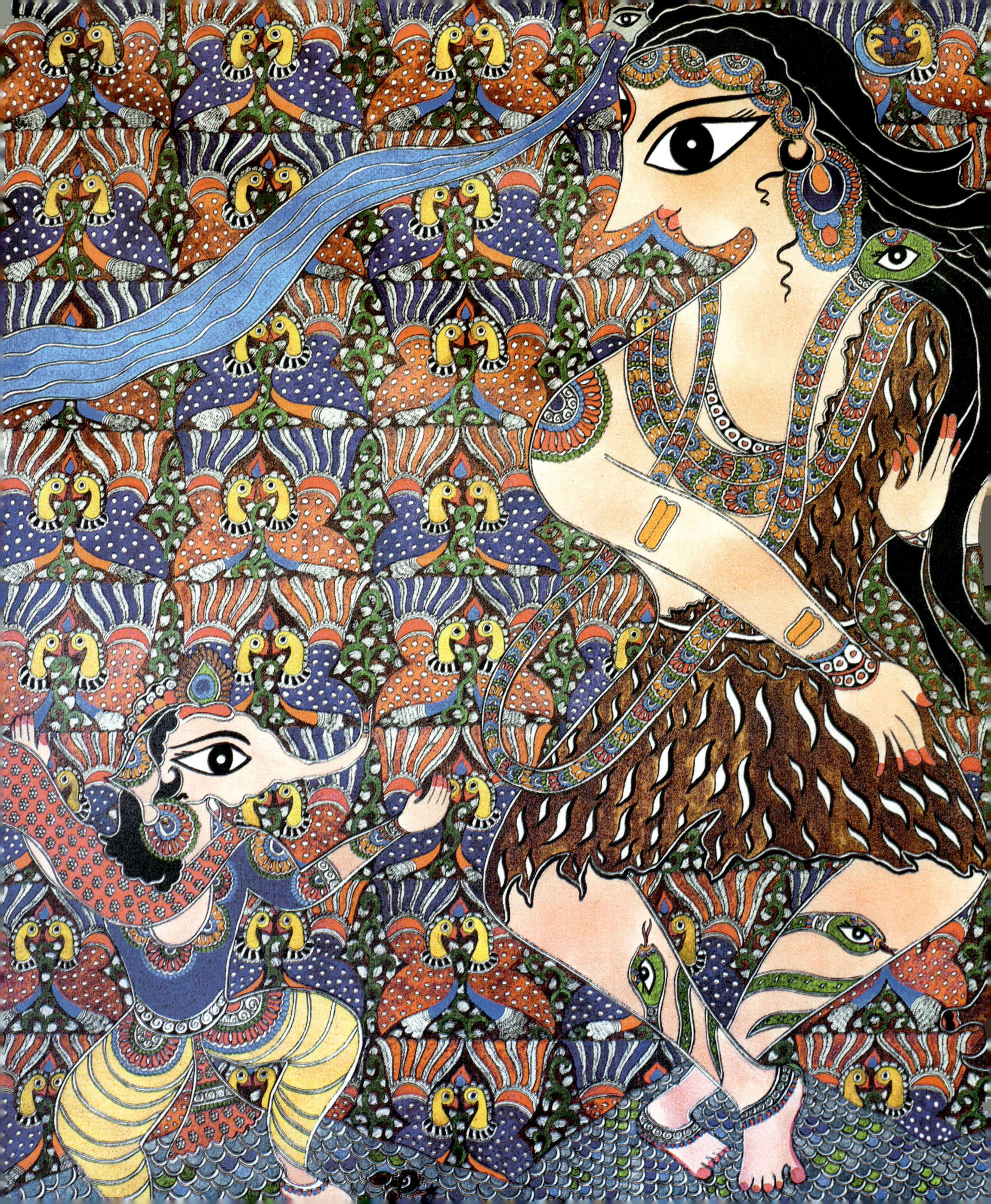

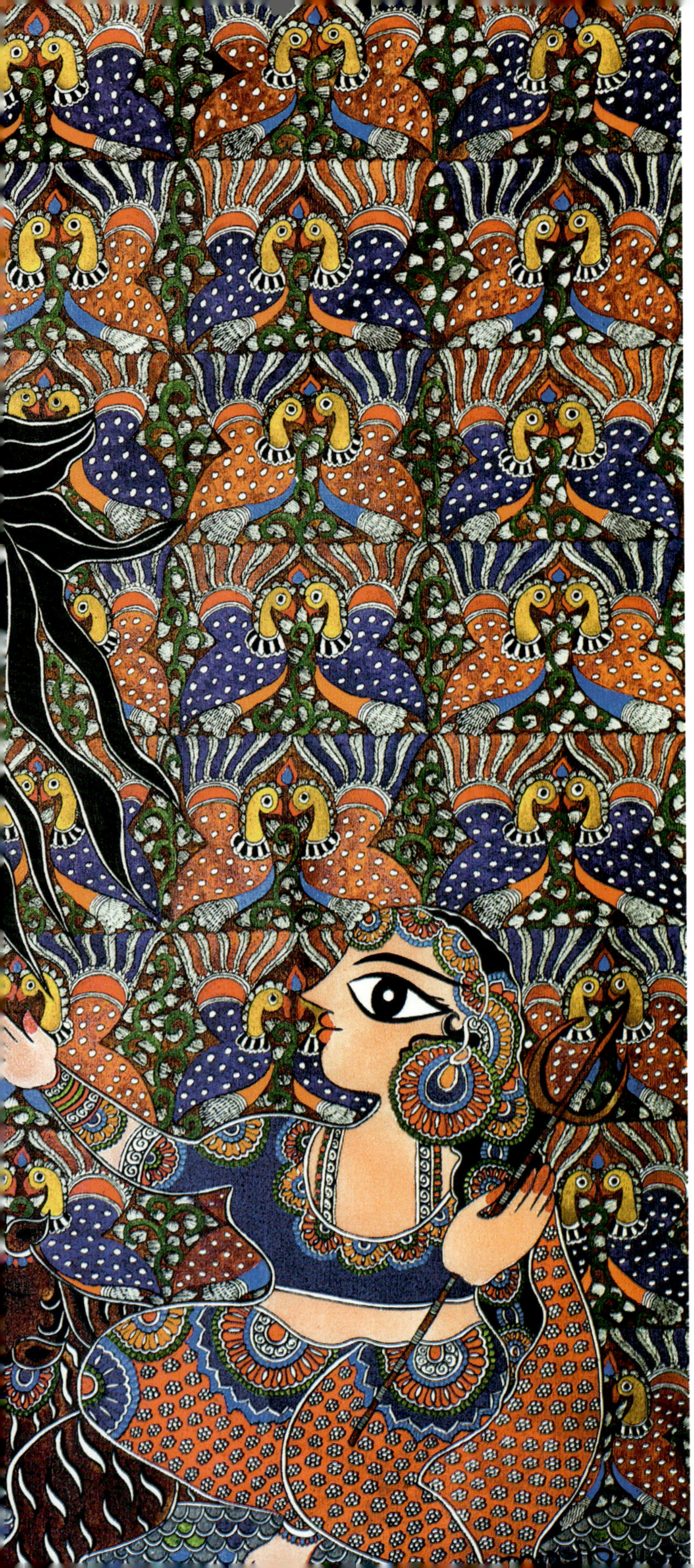

Shiva Dancing with Family
Acrylic on Canvas, 104 x 134 cm

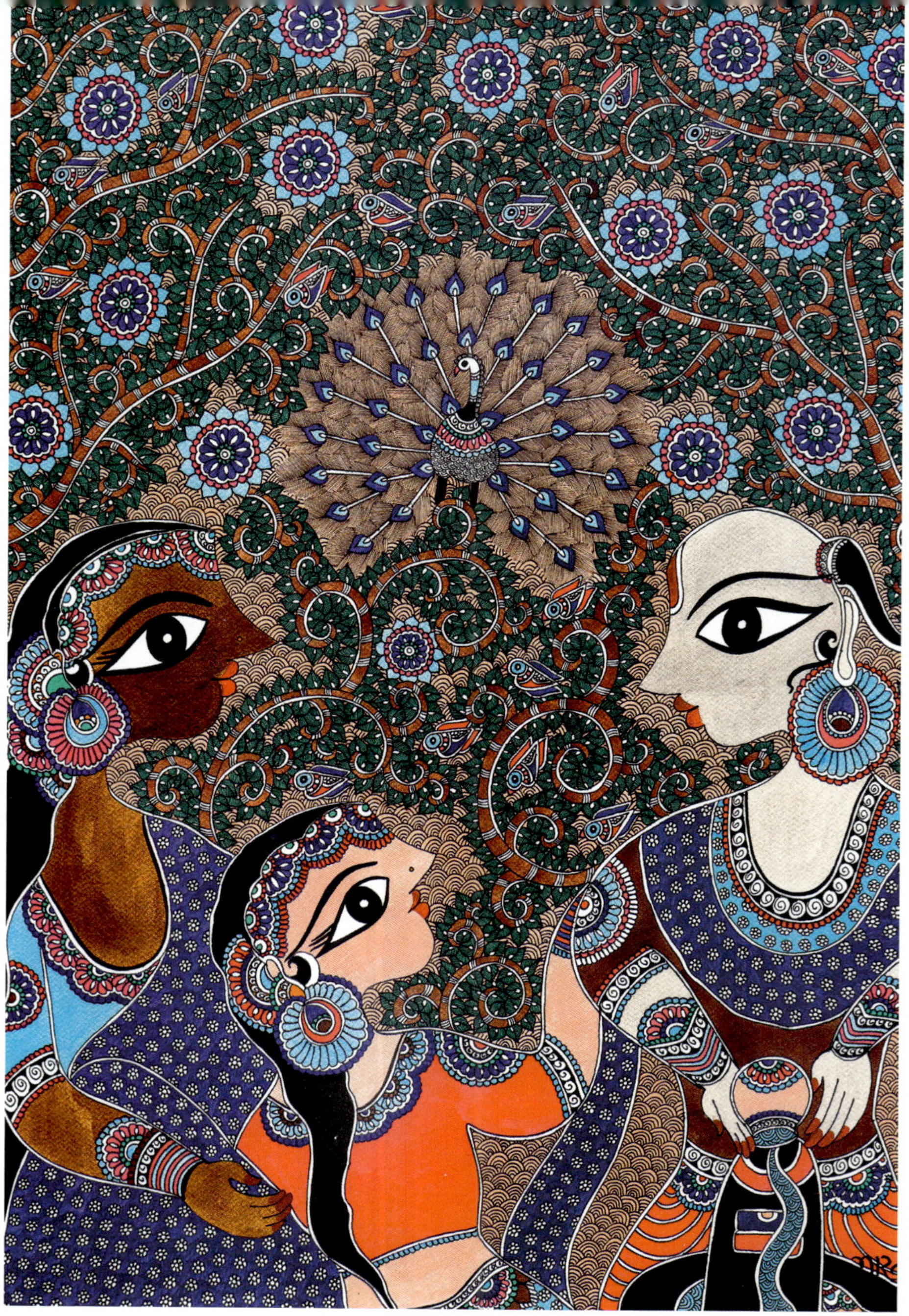

Worship of Shiva-linga
Pigments on Paper, 75 x 55 cm

Shiva, Parvati and Ganesha Around Shiva-linga
Pigments on Paper, 76 x 56 cm (p. 73)

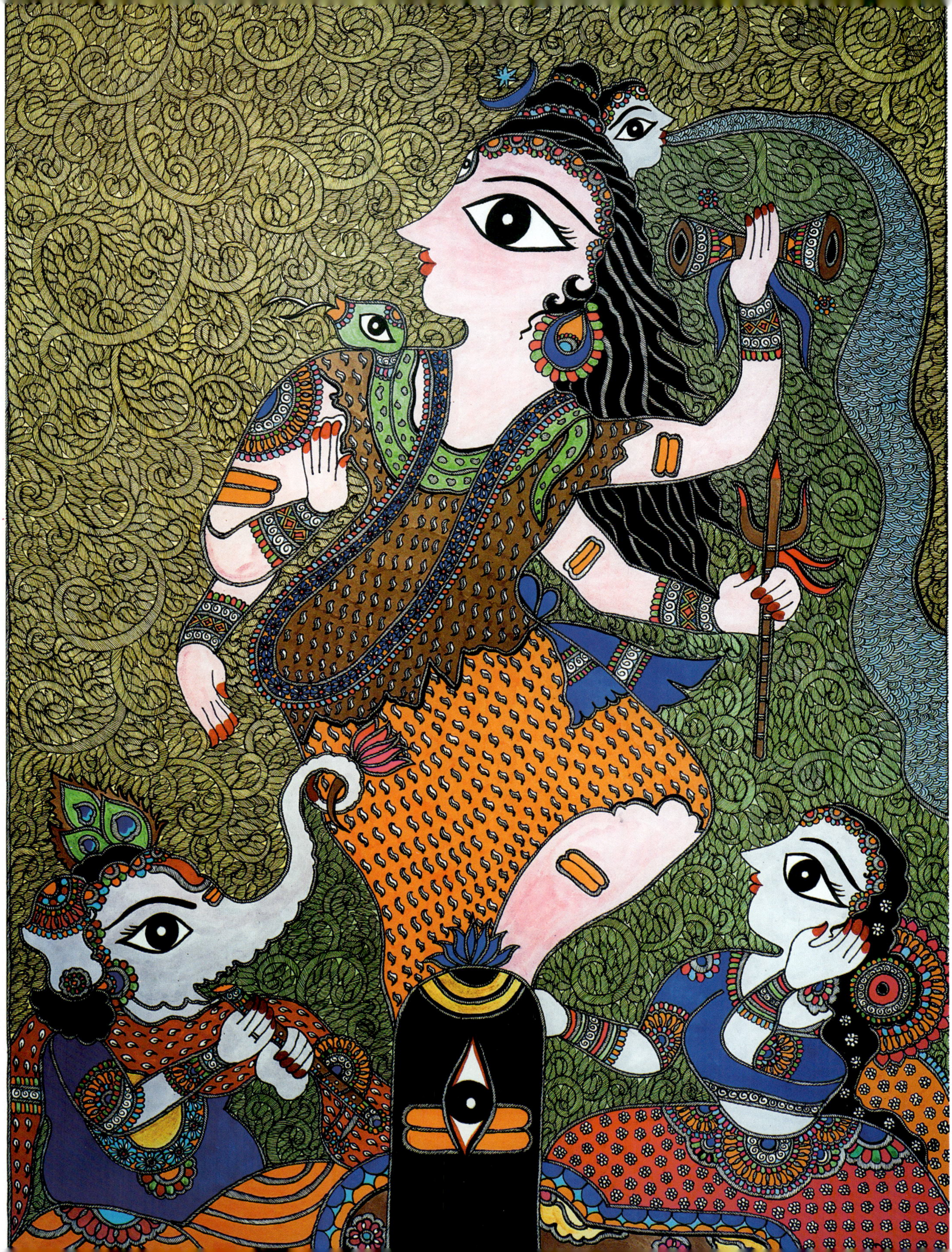

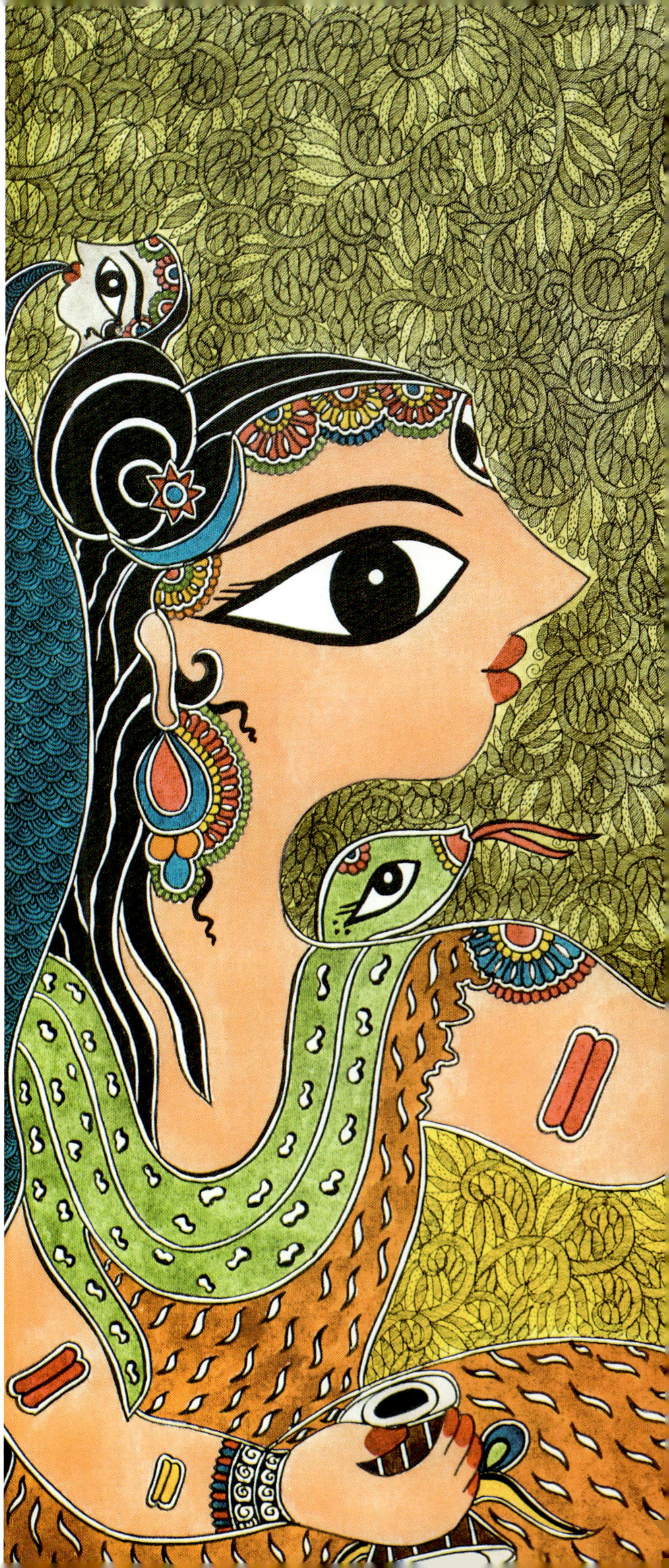

Shiva, Parvati and Nandi
Acrylic on Canvas, 80 x 100 cm

Shiva and His Family with Lotuses
Acrylic on Canvas, 60 x 90 cm
(pp. 76–77)

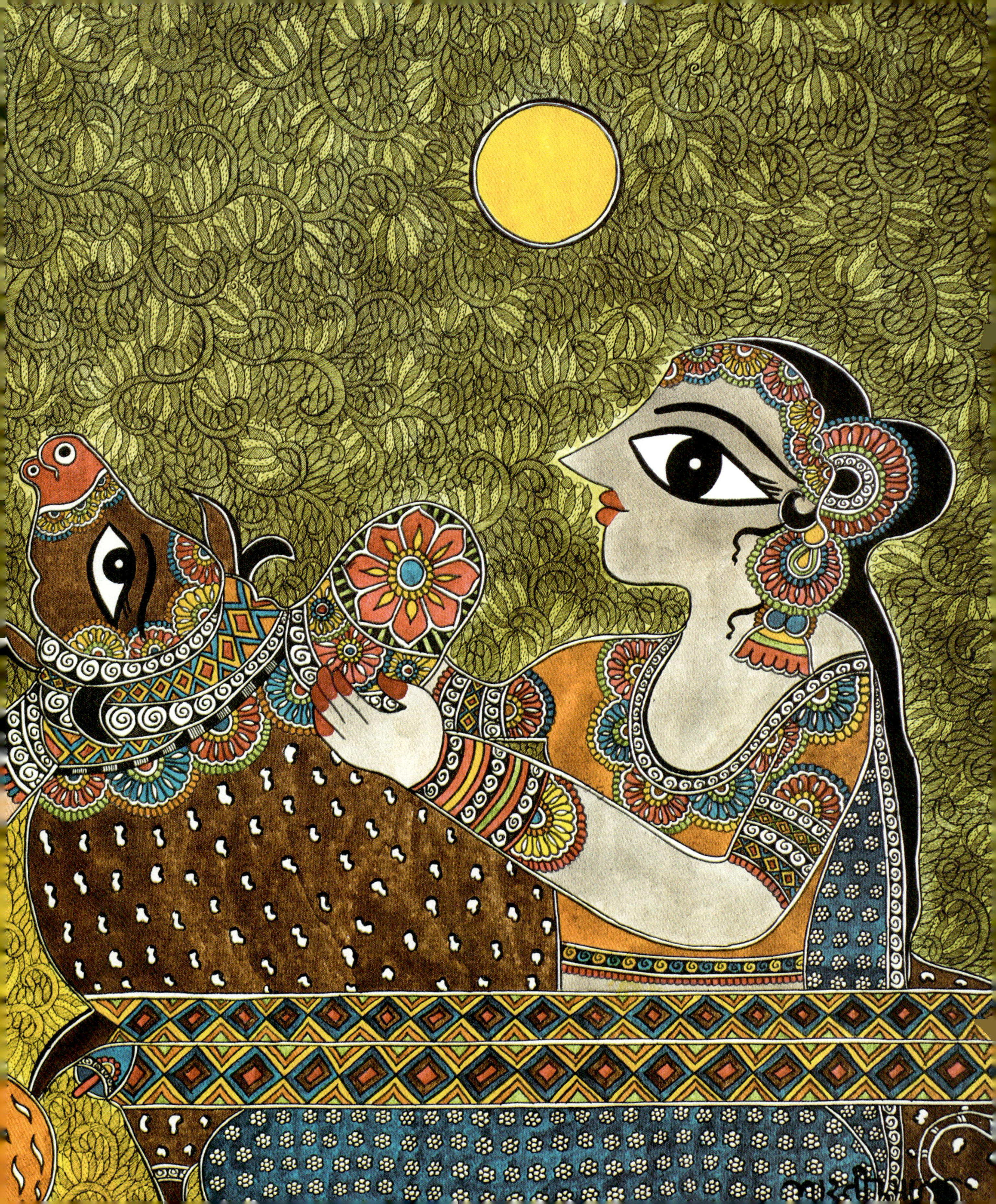

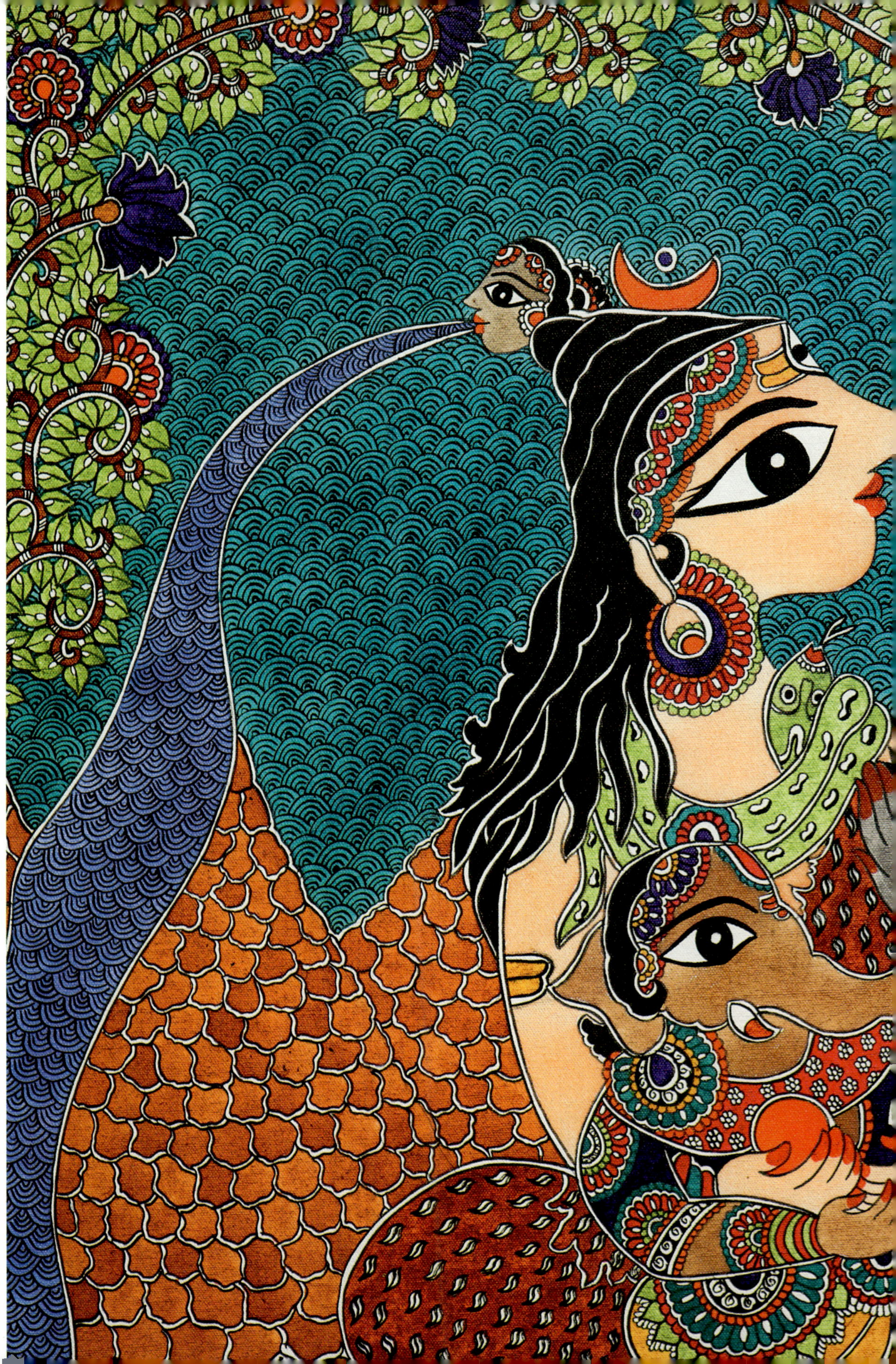

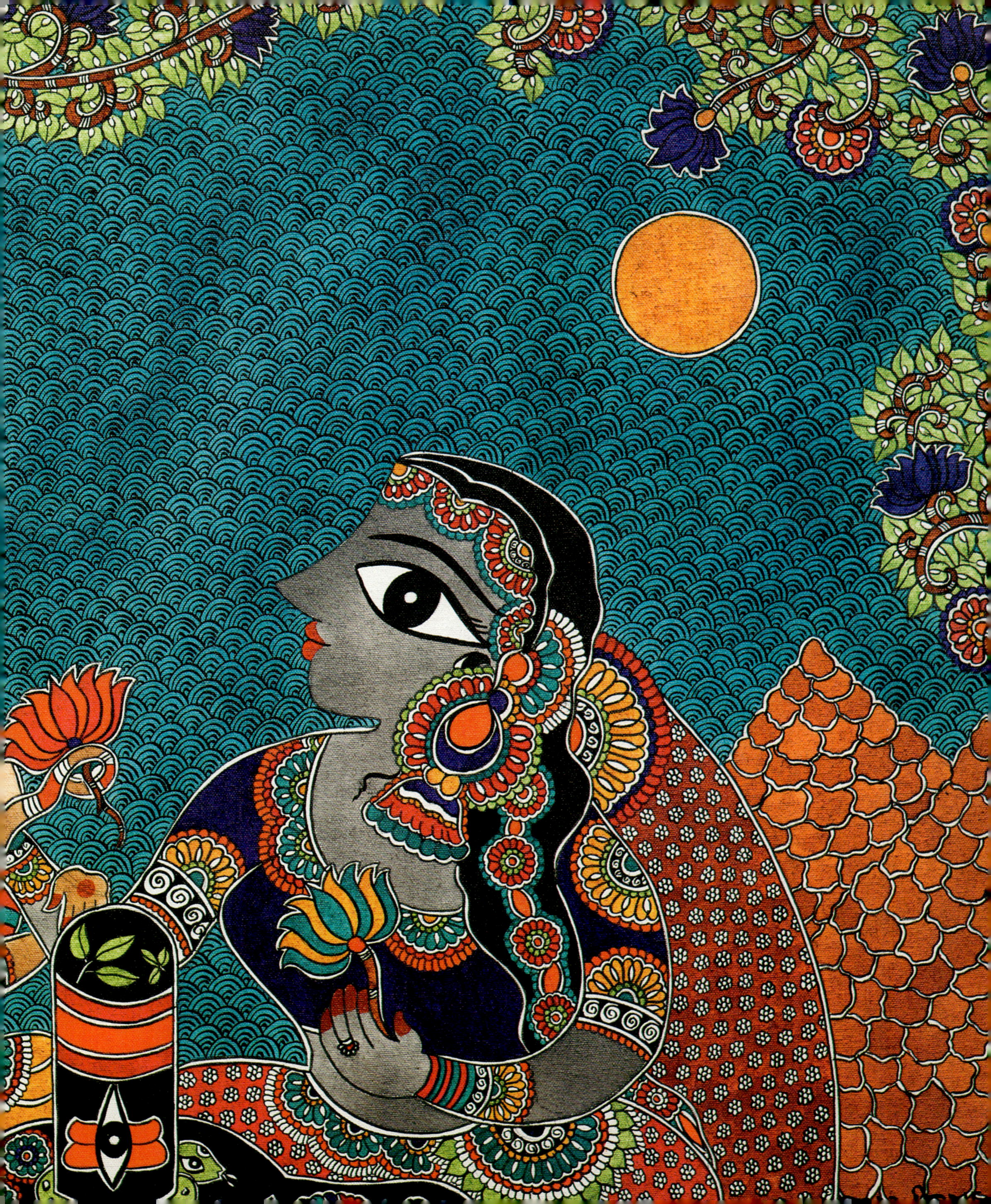

GANESHA

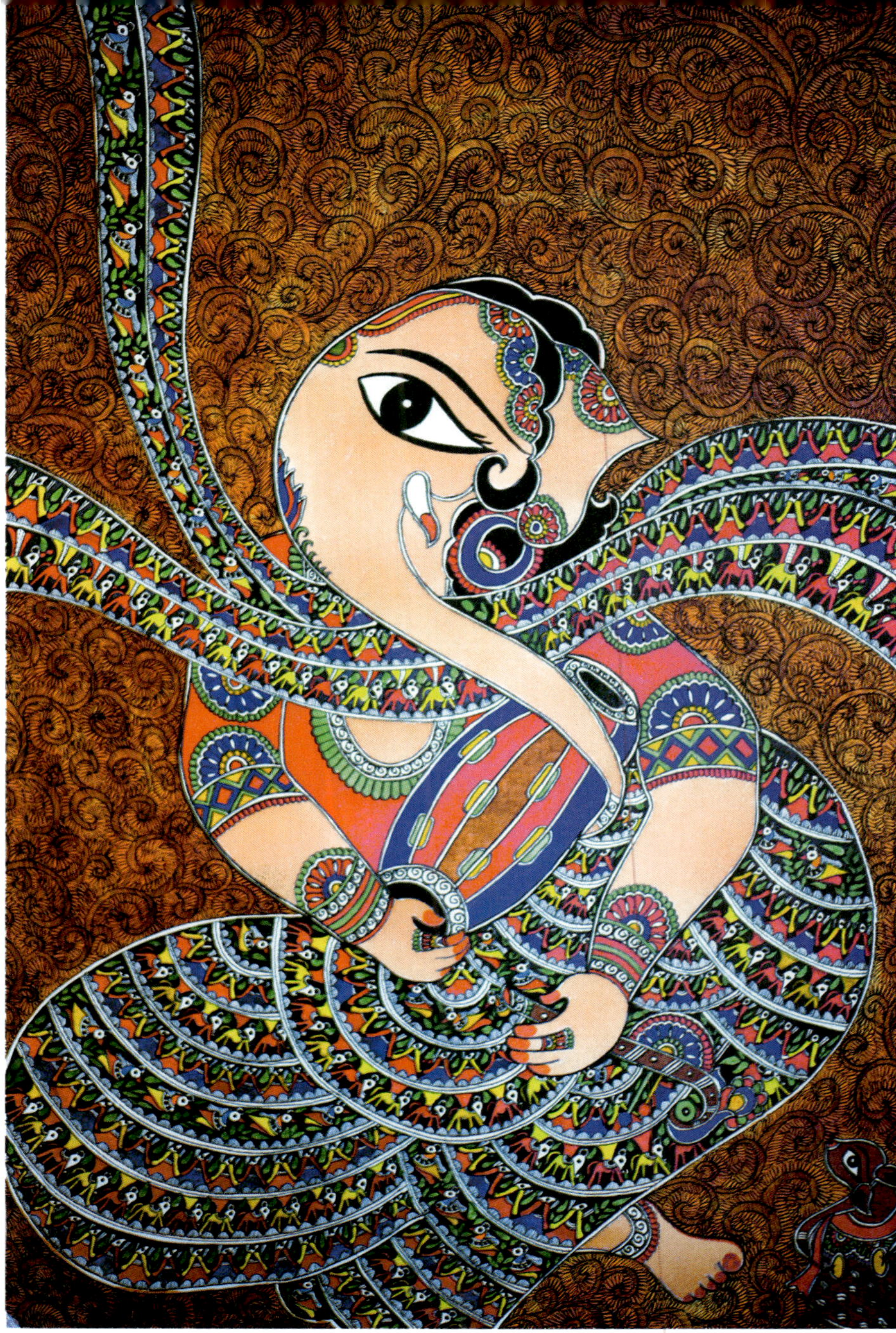

Ganesha Playing Musical Instruments
Acrylic on Canvas, 96 x 70 cm

Ganesha, The Elephant God
Pigments on Paper, 73 x 53 cm (p. 81)

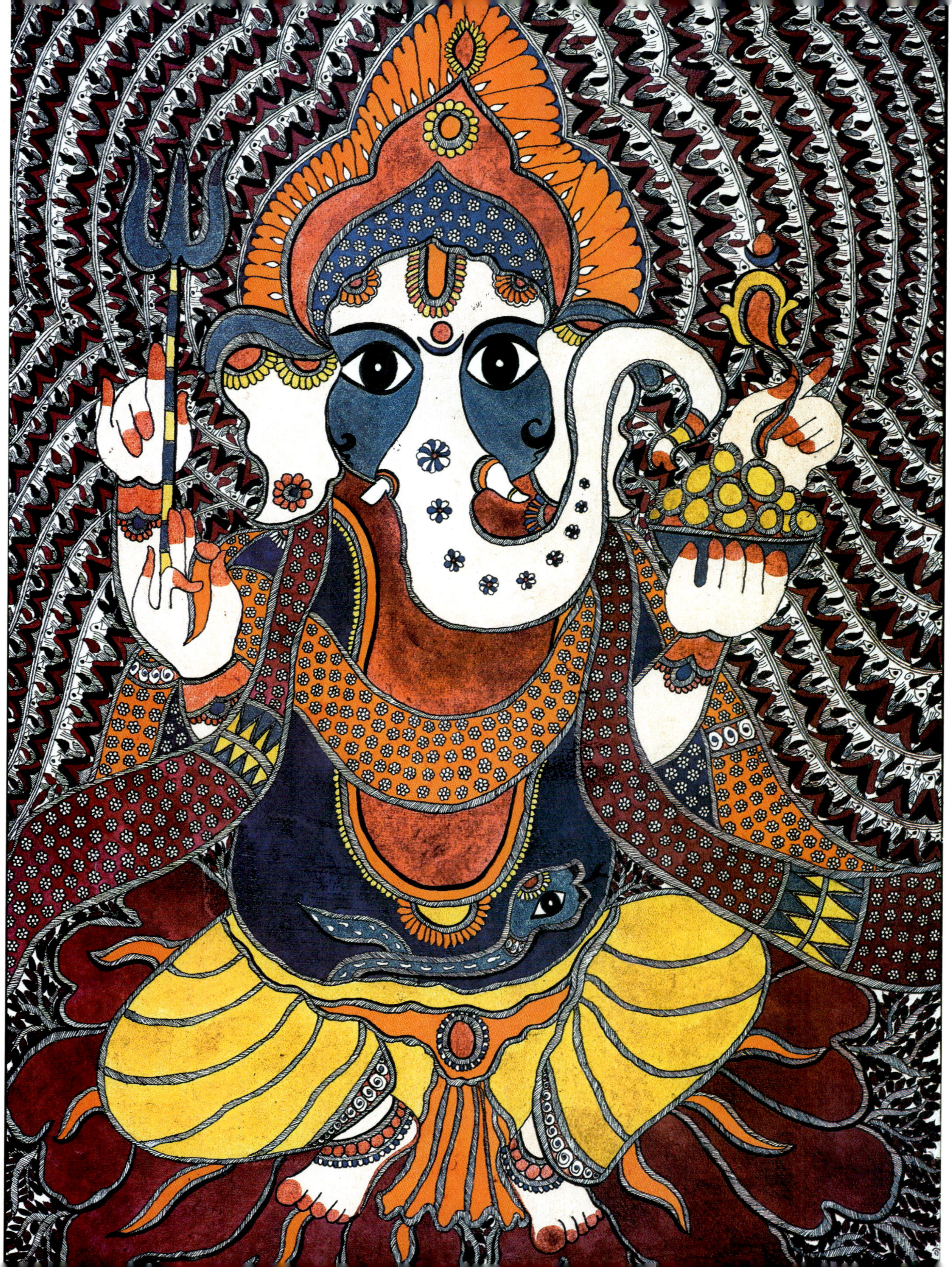

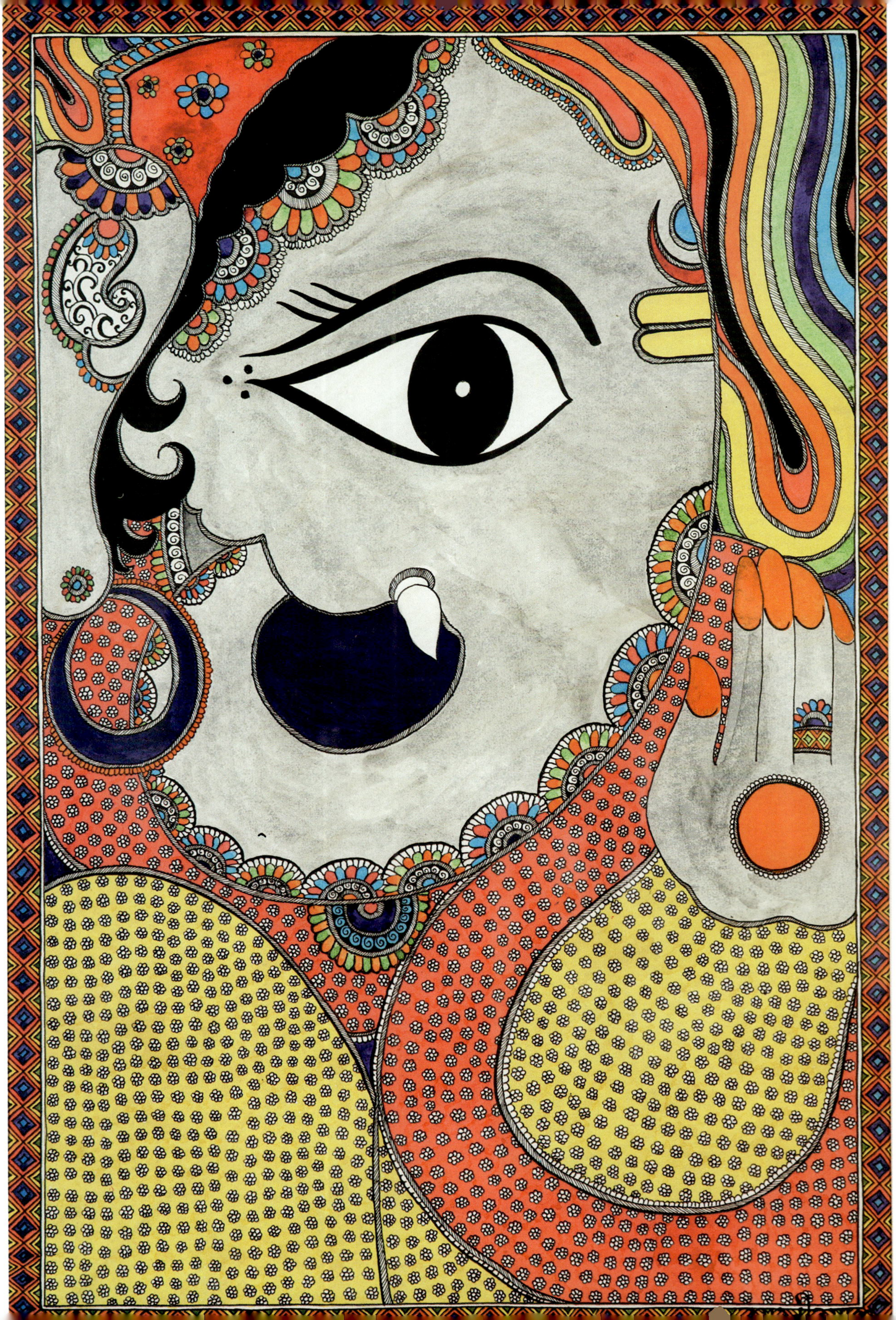

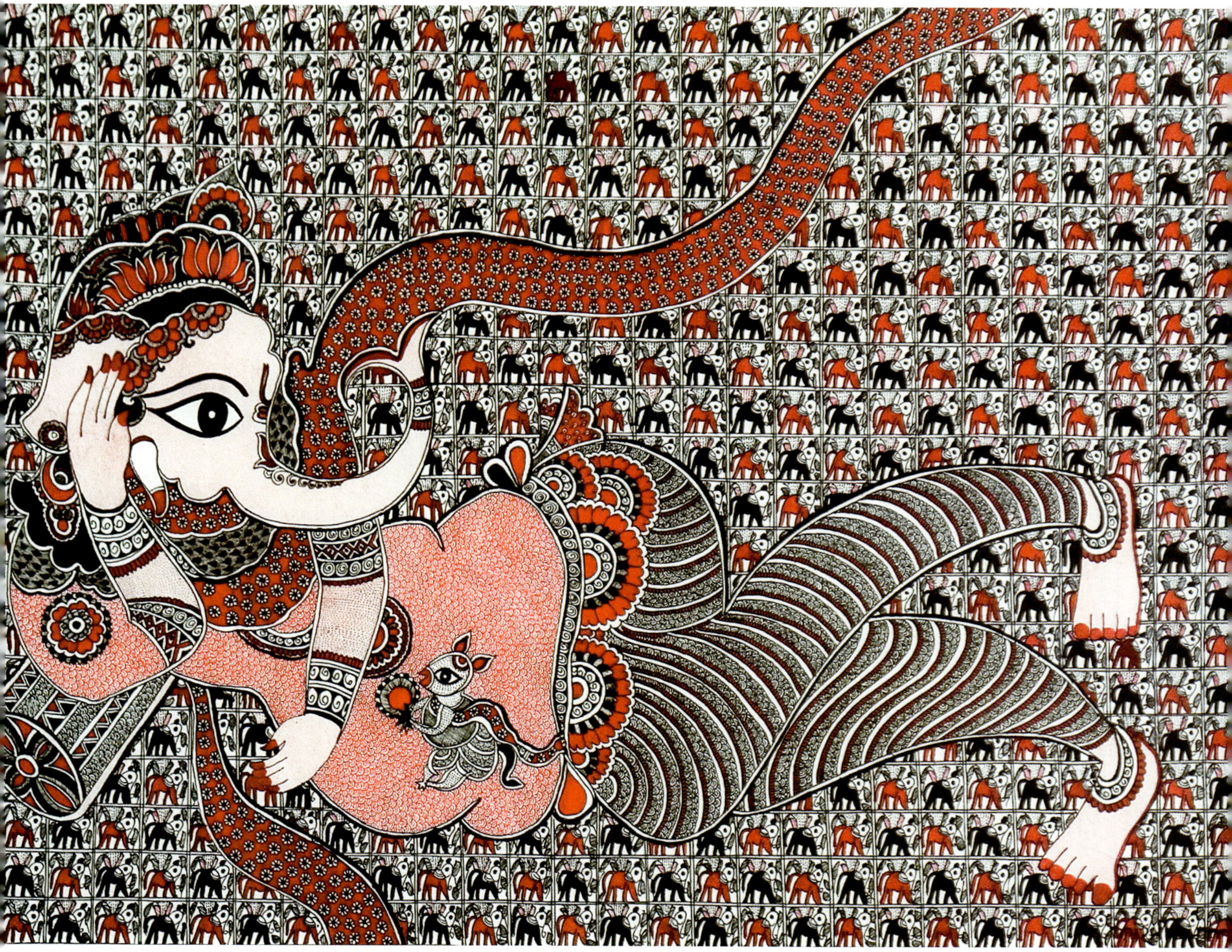

Reclining Ganesha
Pigments on Paper, 58 x 78 cm

Ganesha
Pigments on Paper, 53 x 35 cm (p. 82)

Devi

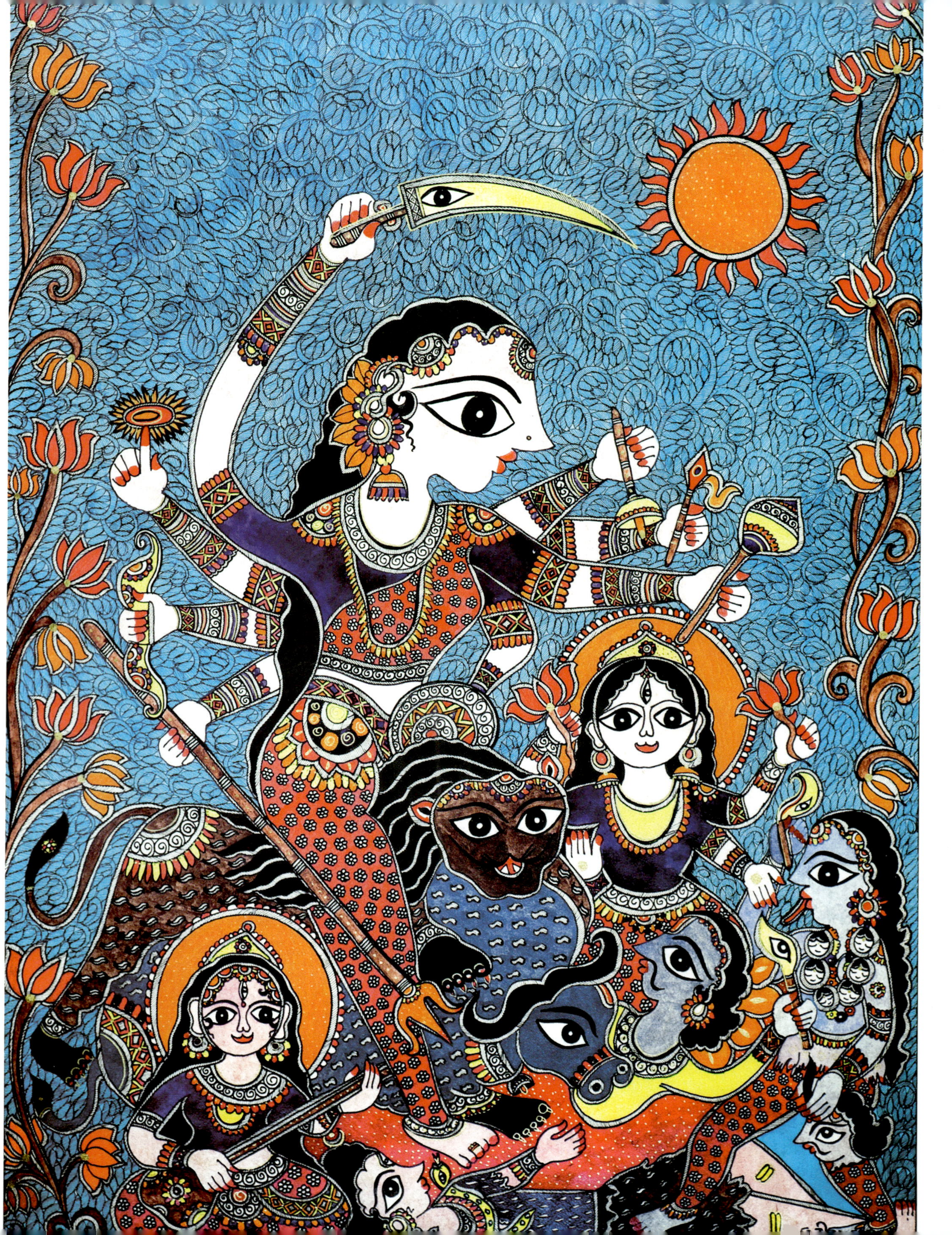

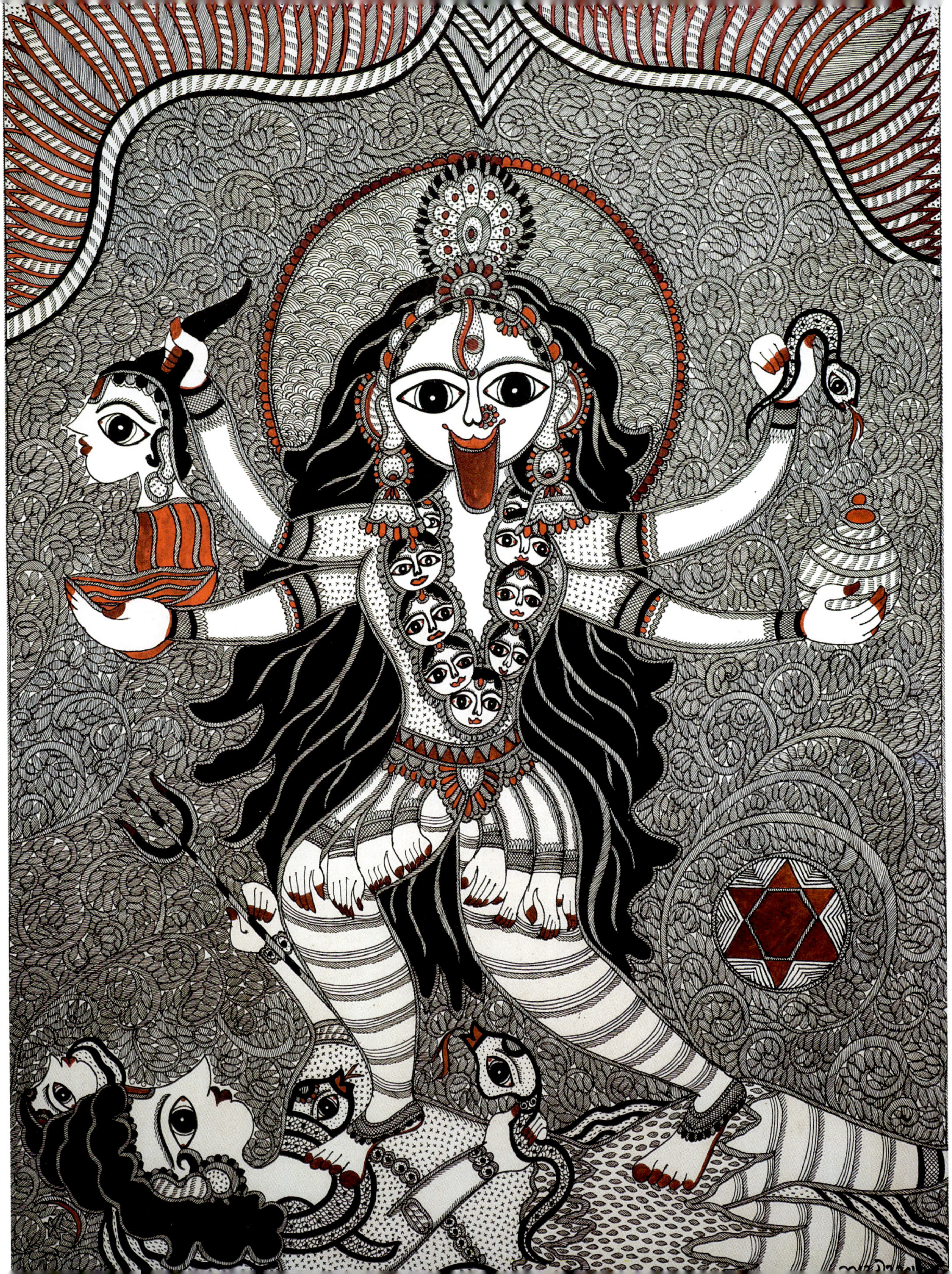

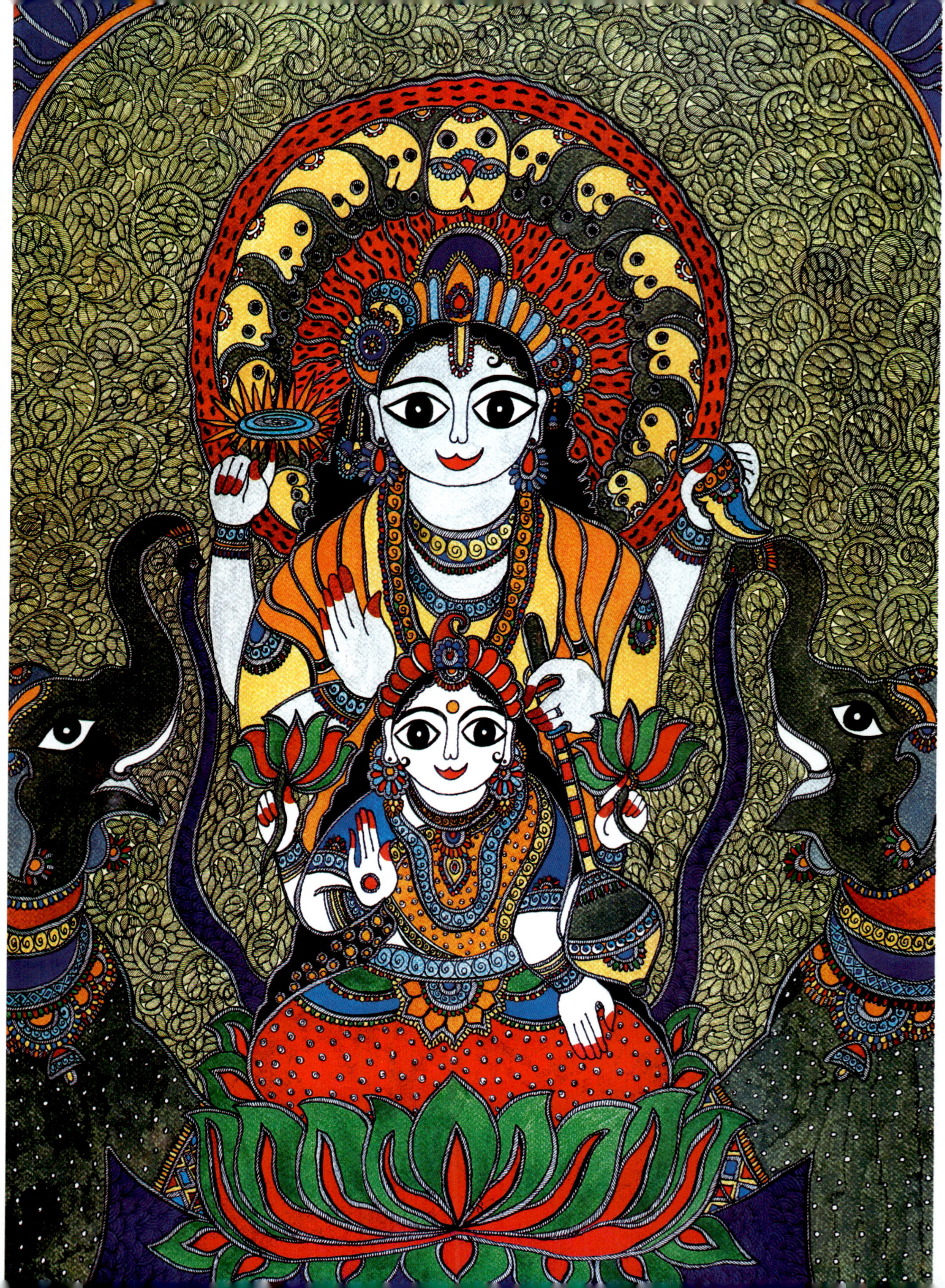

Goddess Durga Punishes Mahishasura
Pigments on Paper, 73 x 53 cm (p. 86)

Ferocious Goddess Kali Displays Her Weapons
Pigments on Paper, 73 x 53 cm (p. 87)

Lakshmi-Narayan
Pigments on Paper, 74 x 54 cm (p. 88)

The Mahabharata

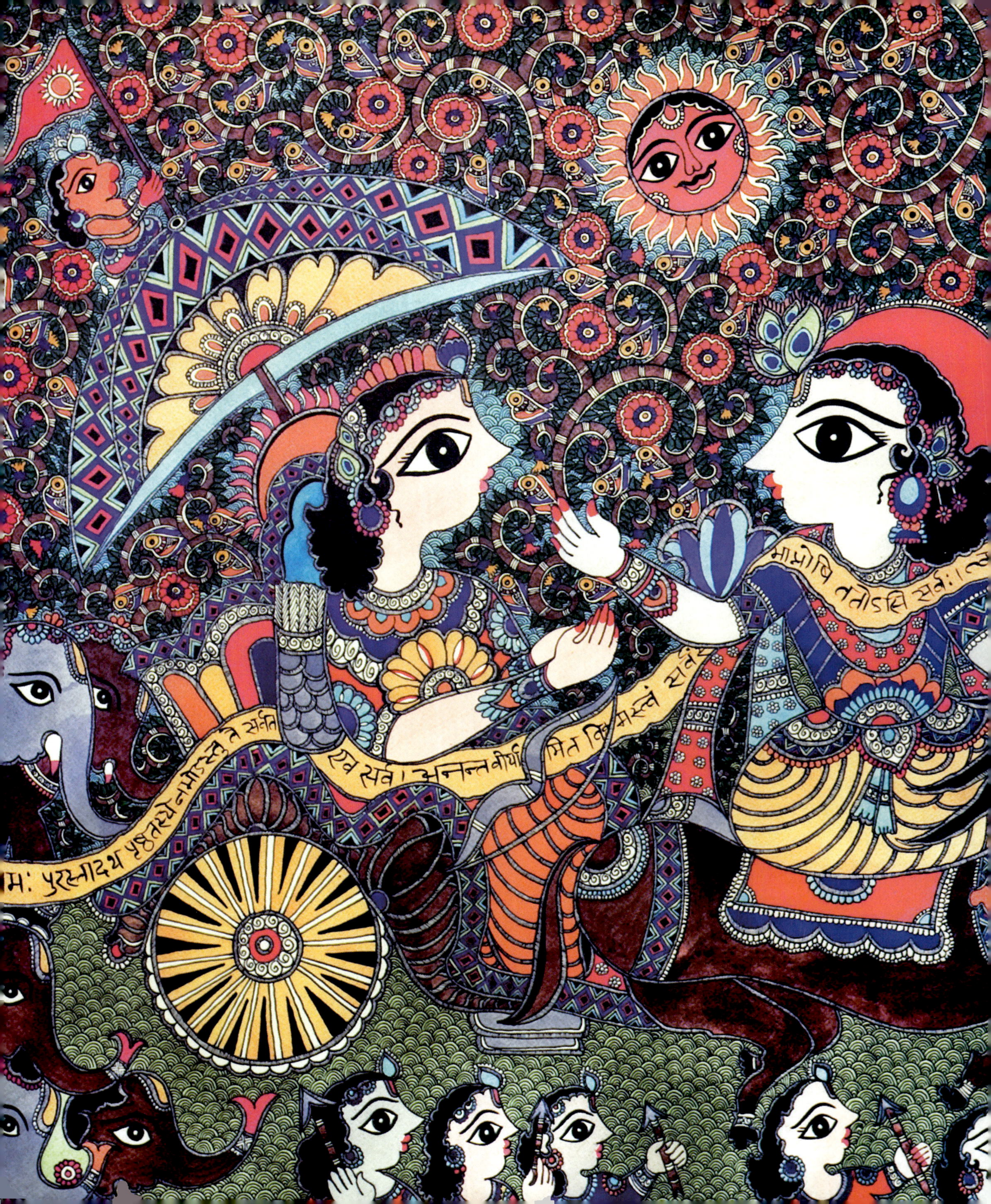
मः पुरस्तादथ पृष्ठतस्ते नमोऽस्तु ते सर्वत
एव सर्व। अनन्तवीर्या
मित विक्रमस्त्वं सर्वं
माप्नोषि ततोऽसि सर्वः।

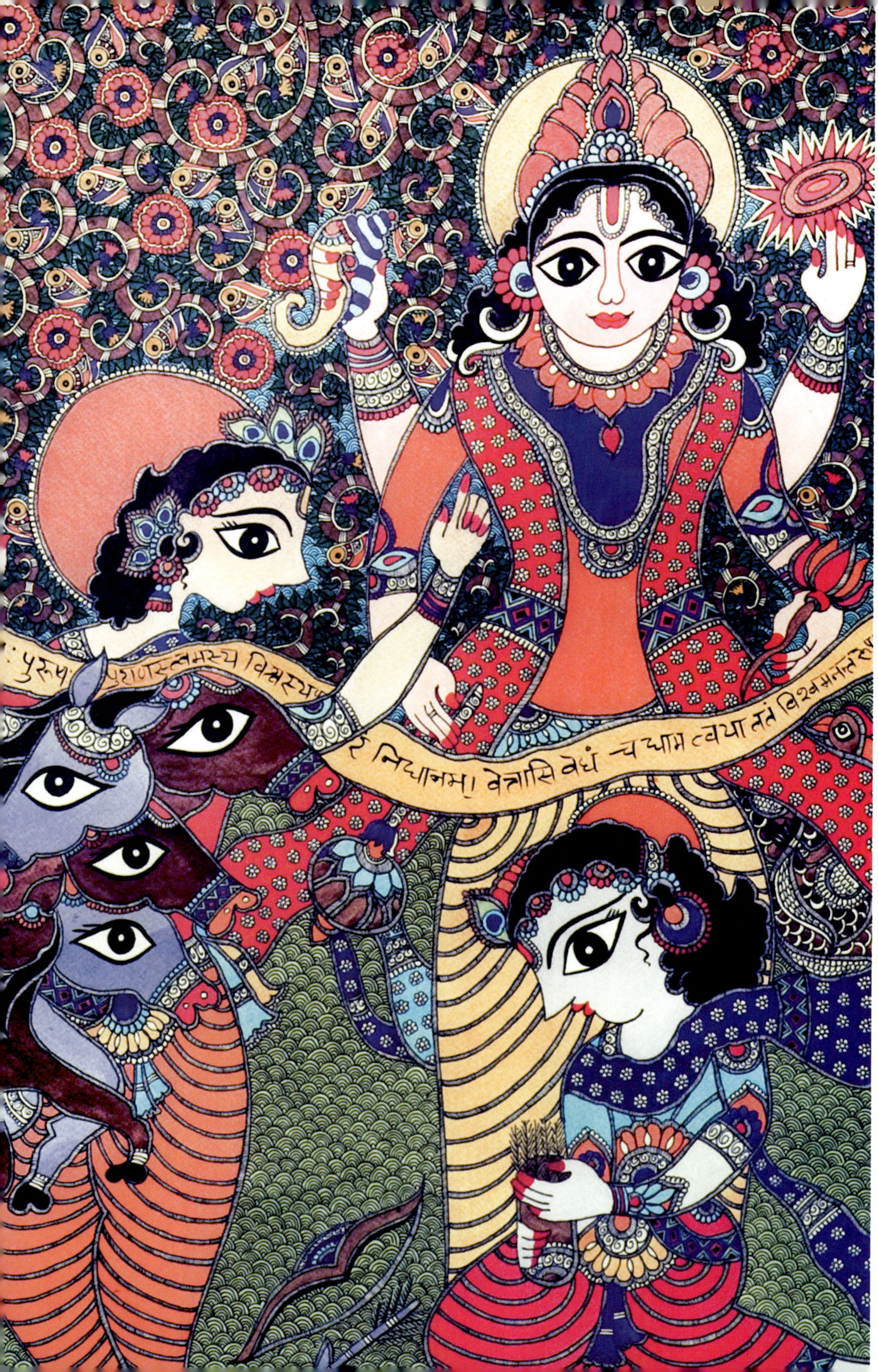
निधानम। वेत्तासि वेधं च धाम त्वया ततं विश्वमनन्त

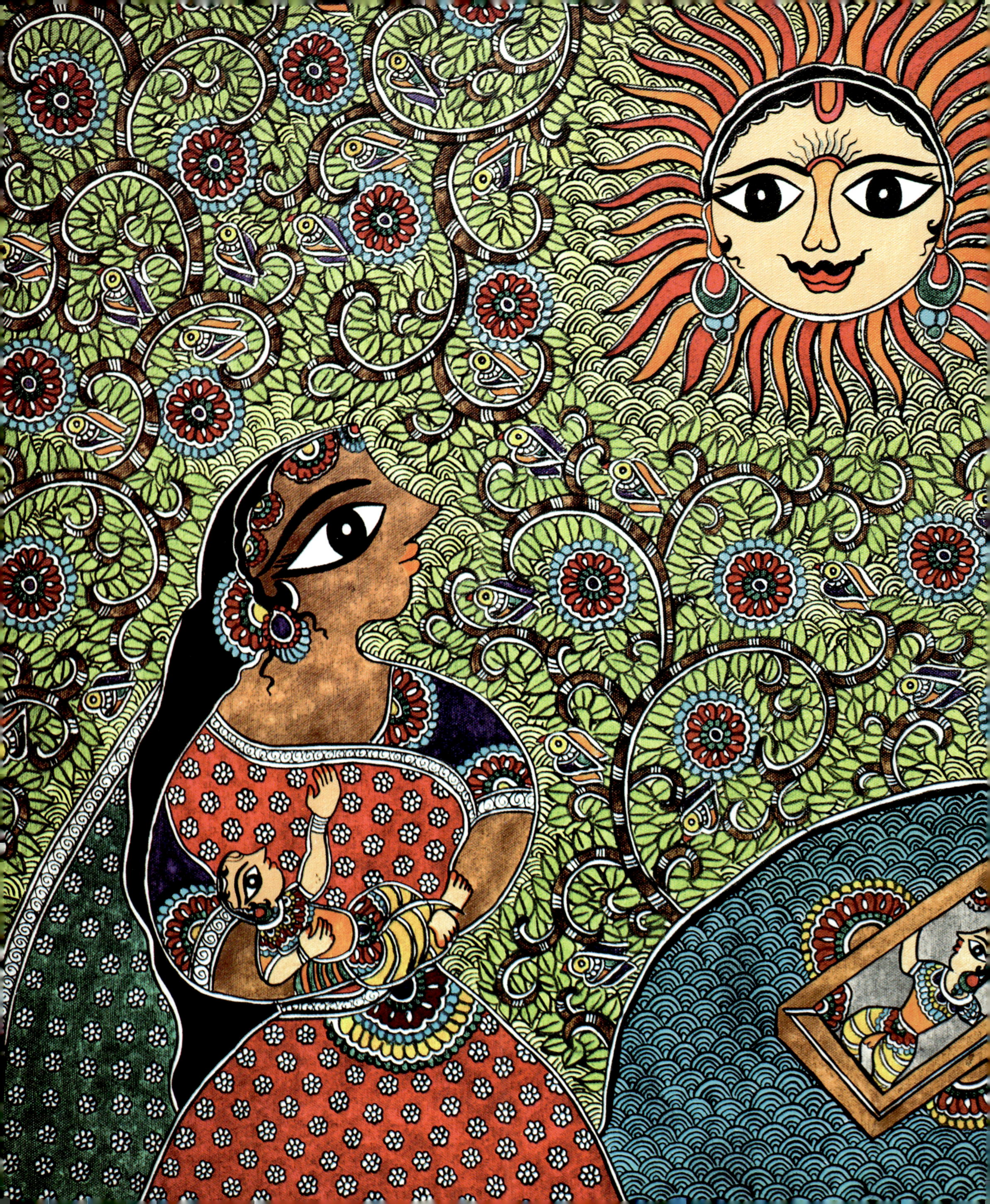

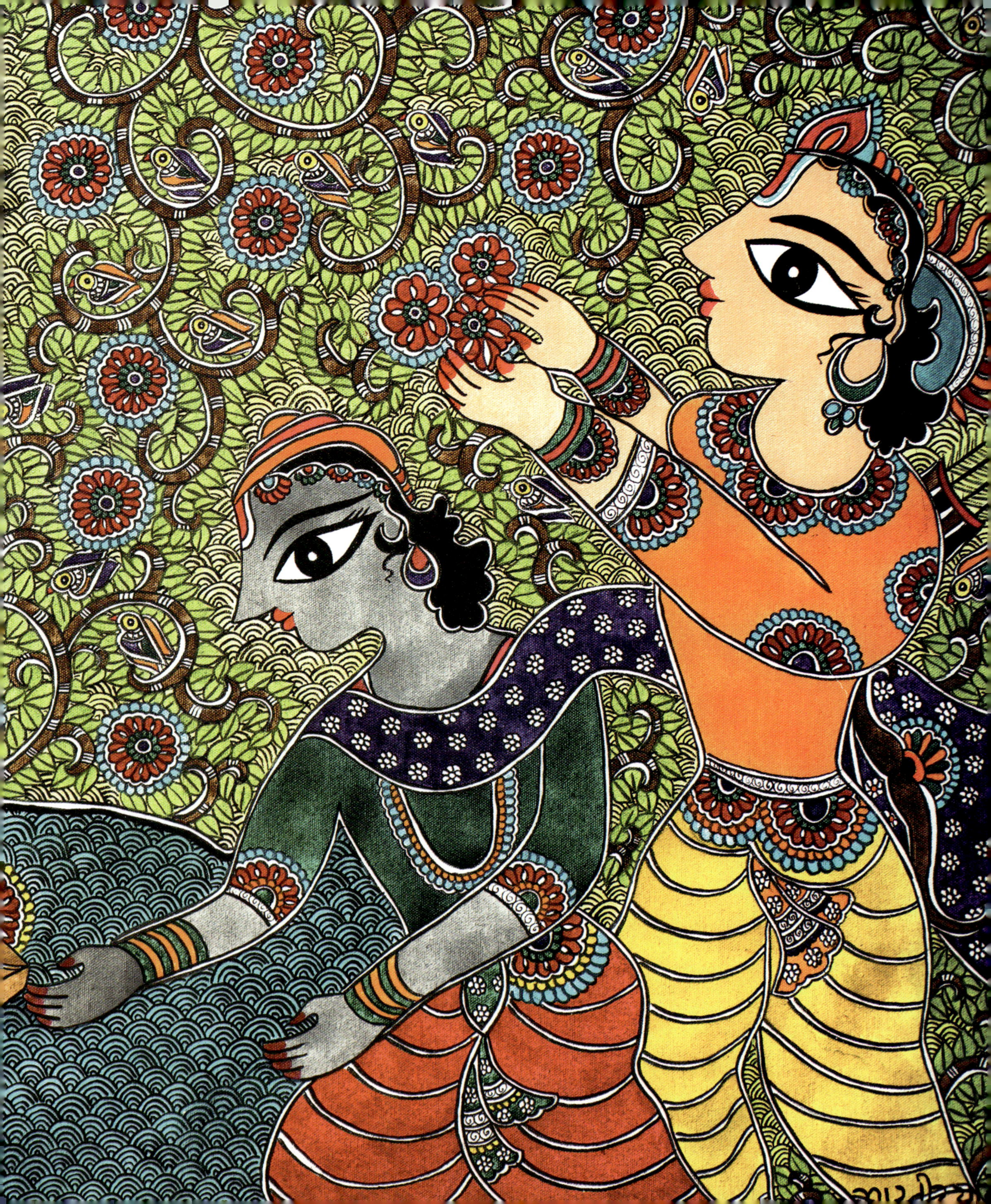

Bhishma on The Bed of Arrows
Acrylic on Canvas, 67 x 82 cm

The Birth of Karna
Acrylic on Canvas, 100 x 60 cm (pp. 94-95)

Krishna and Arjuna
Pigments on Paper, 72 x 105 cm (pp. 92–93)

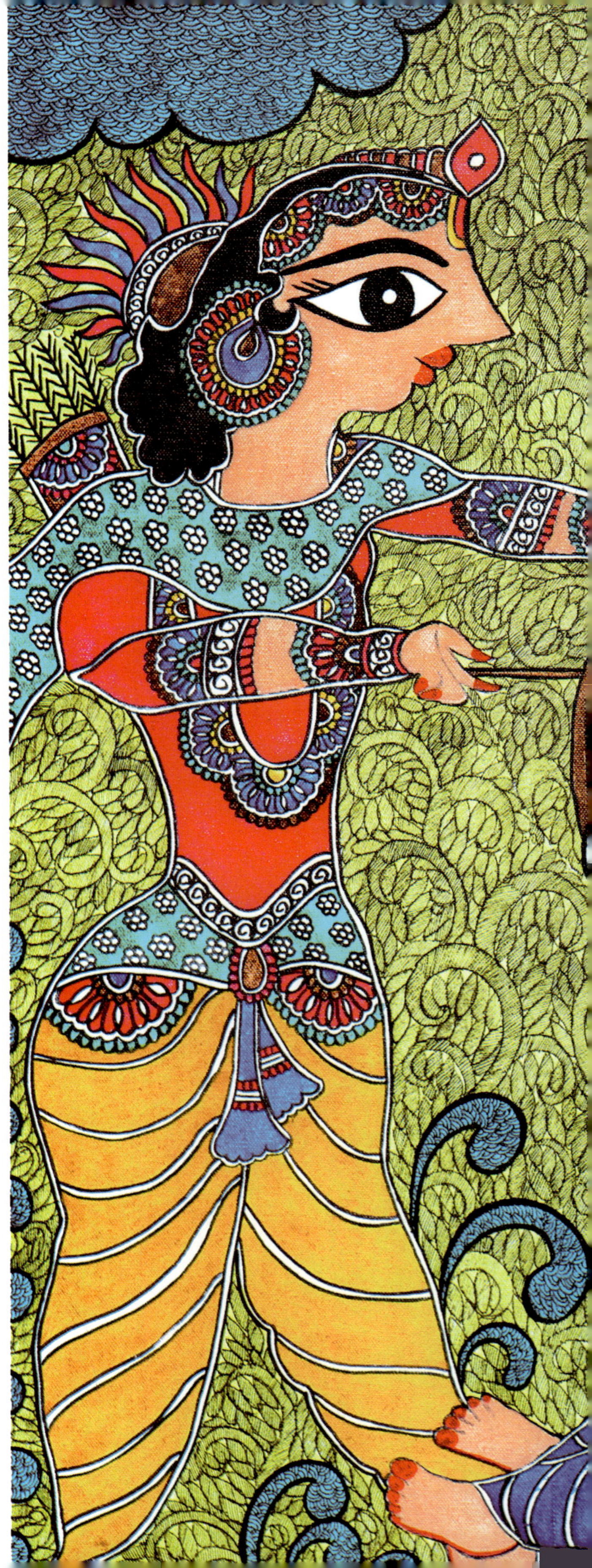

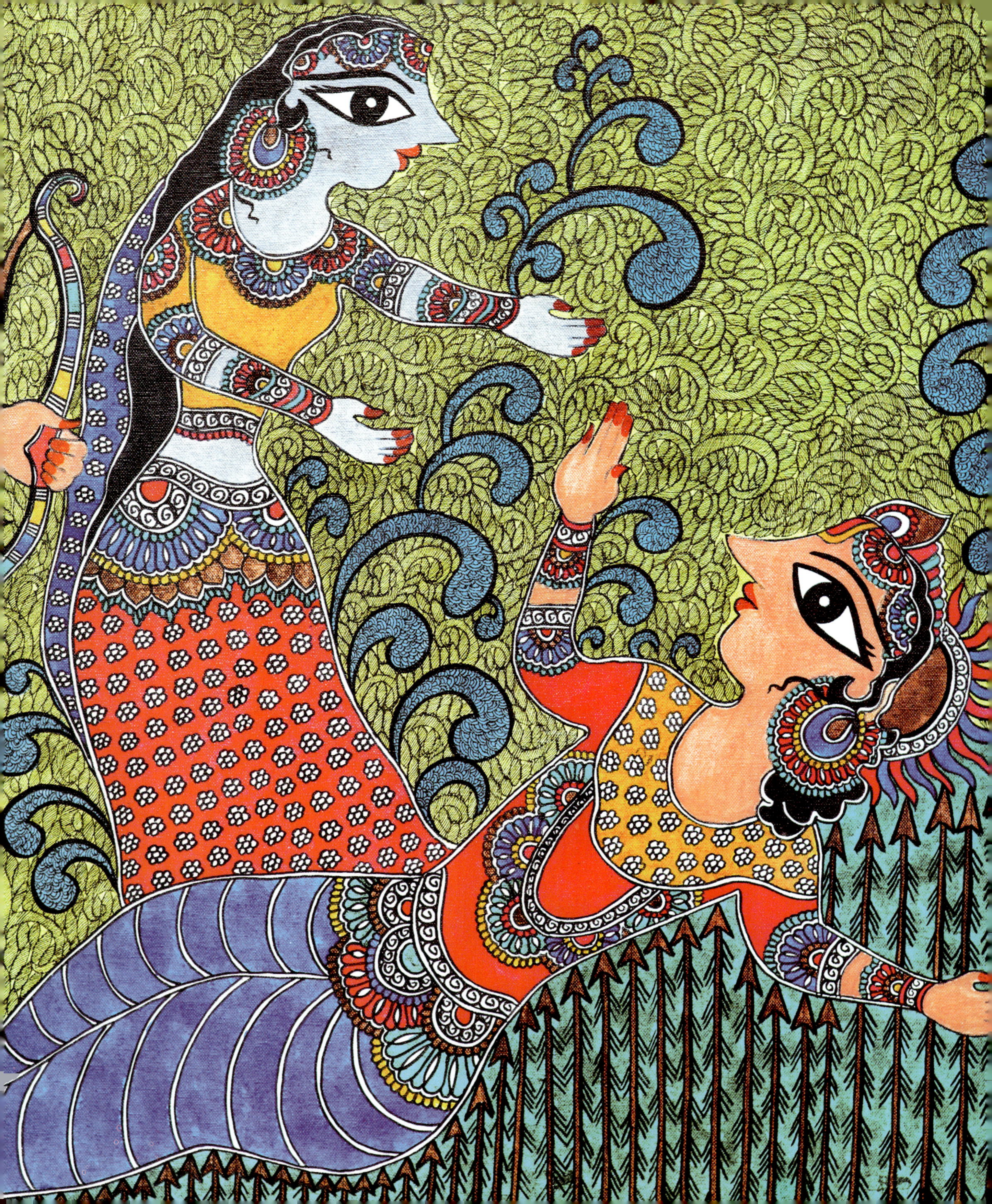

Nature

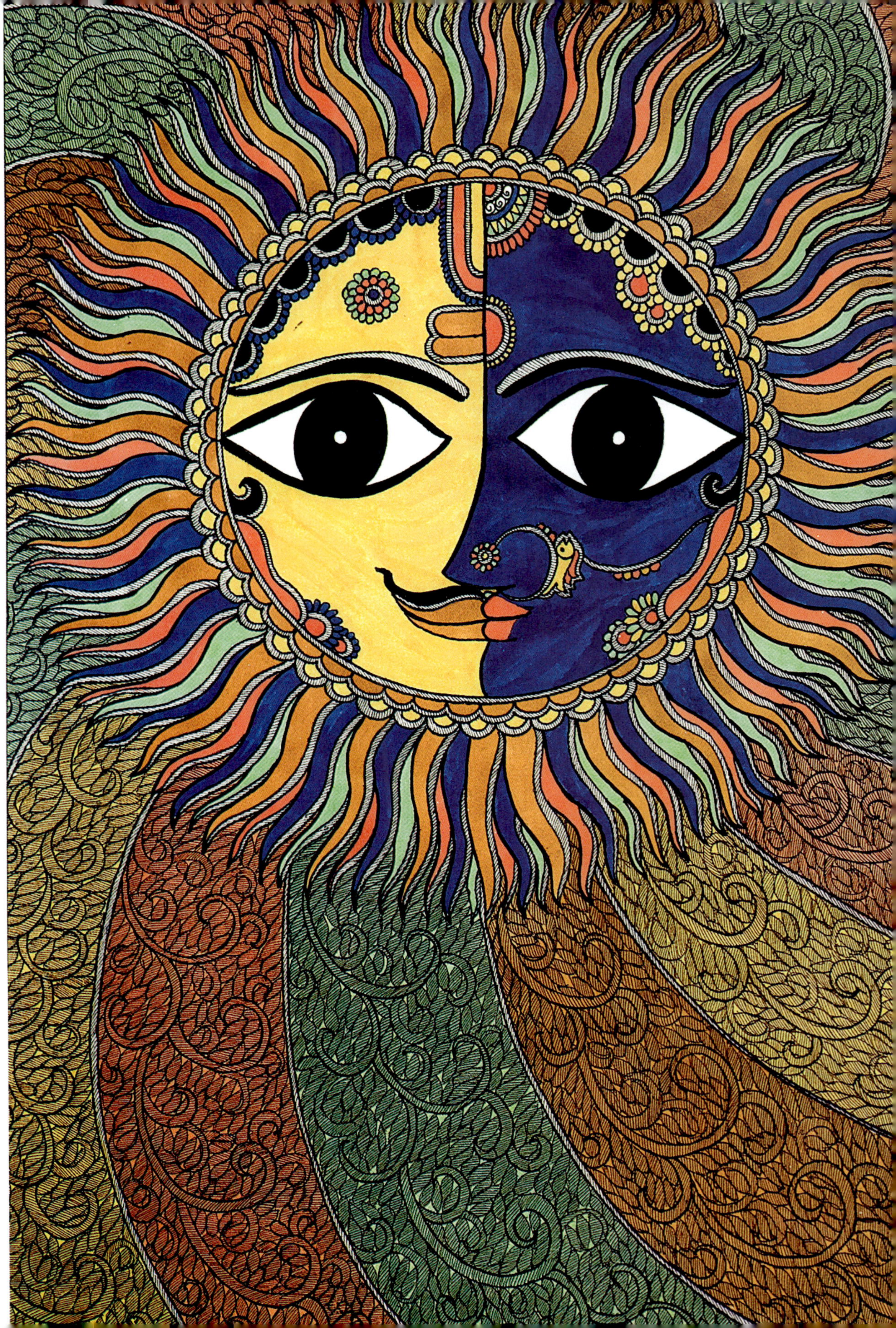

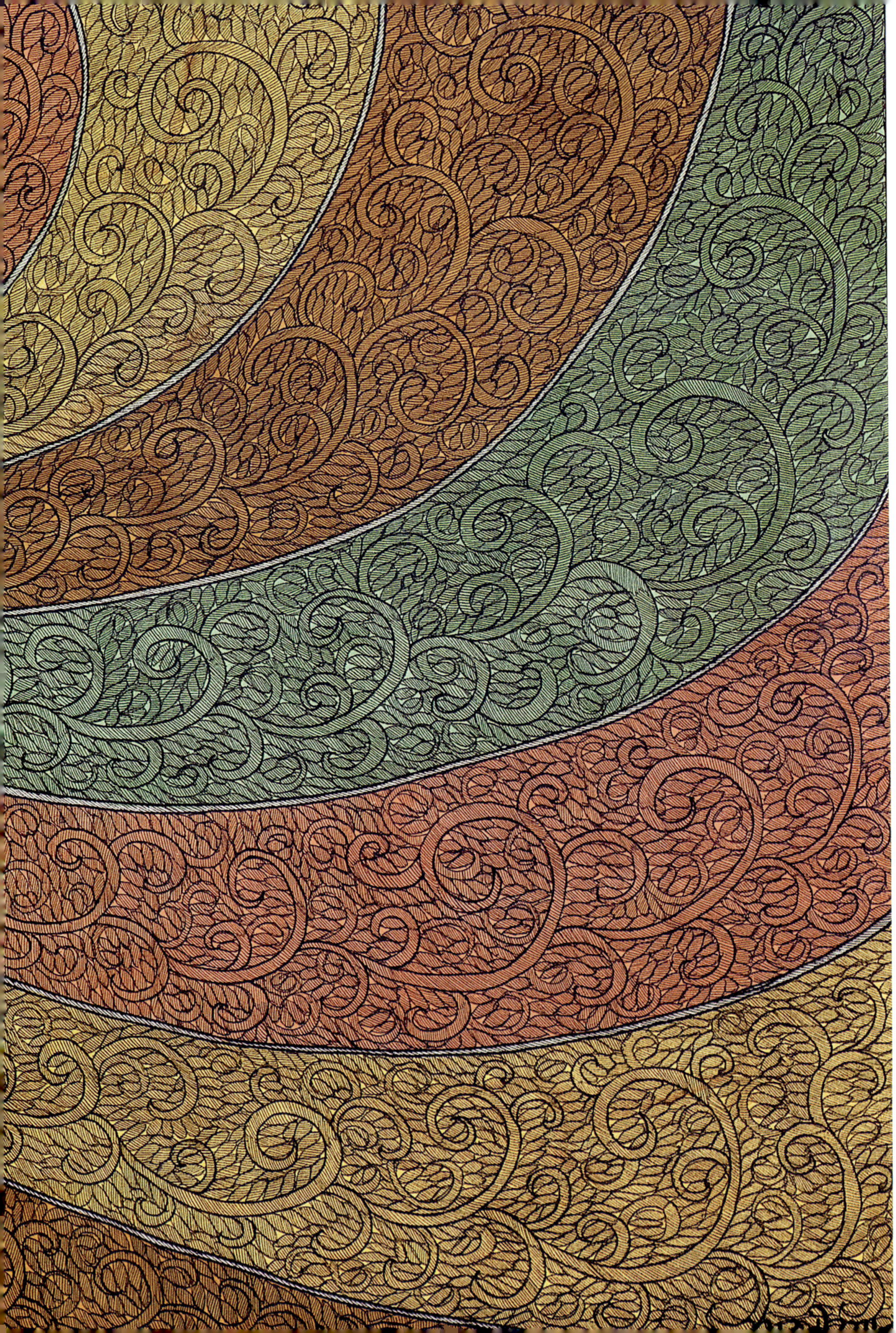

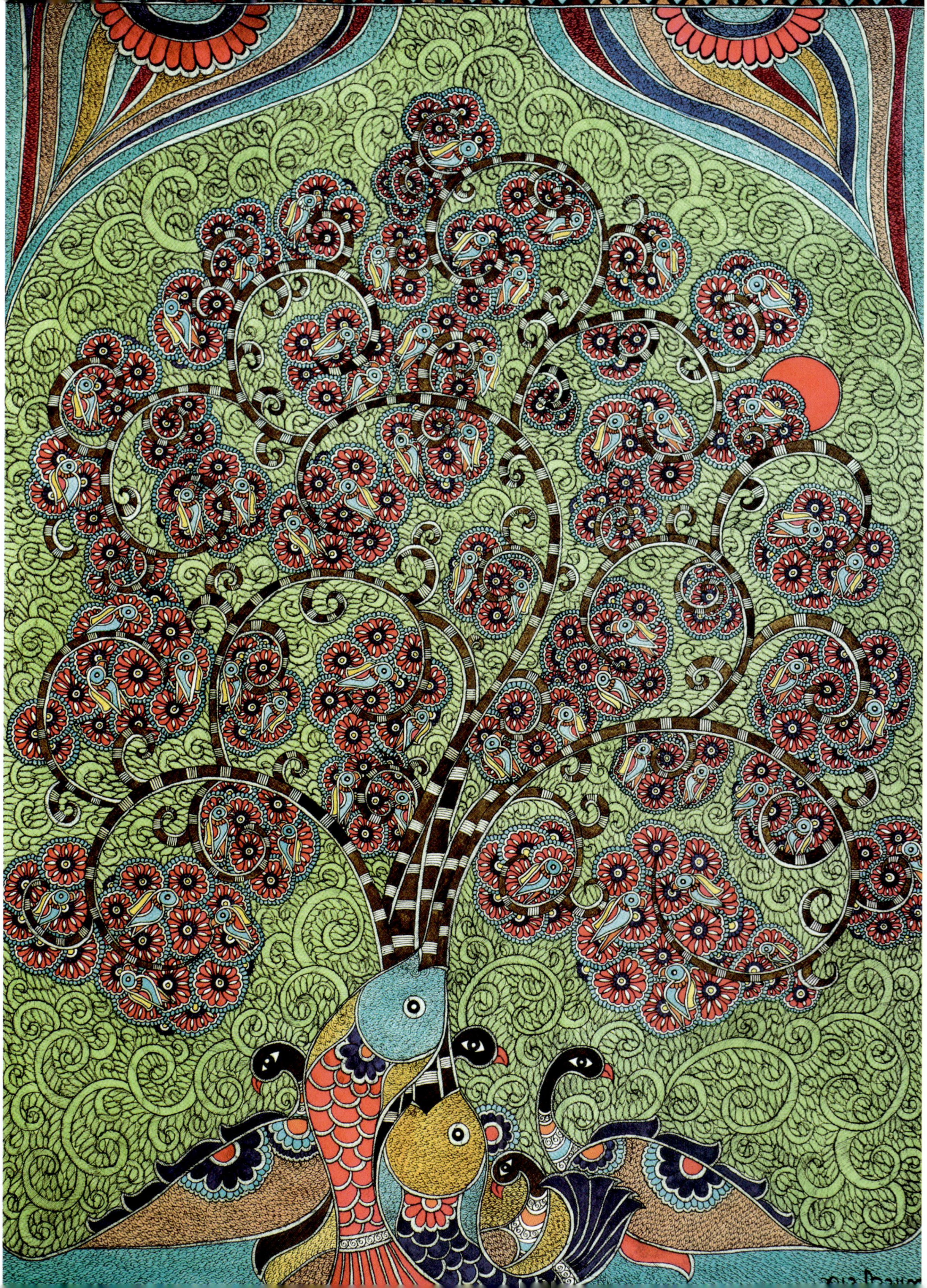

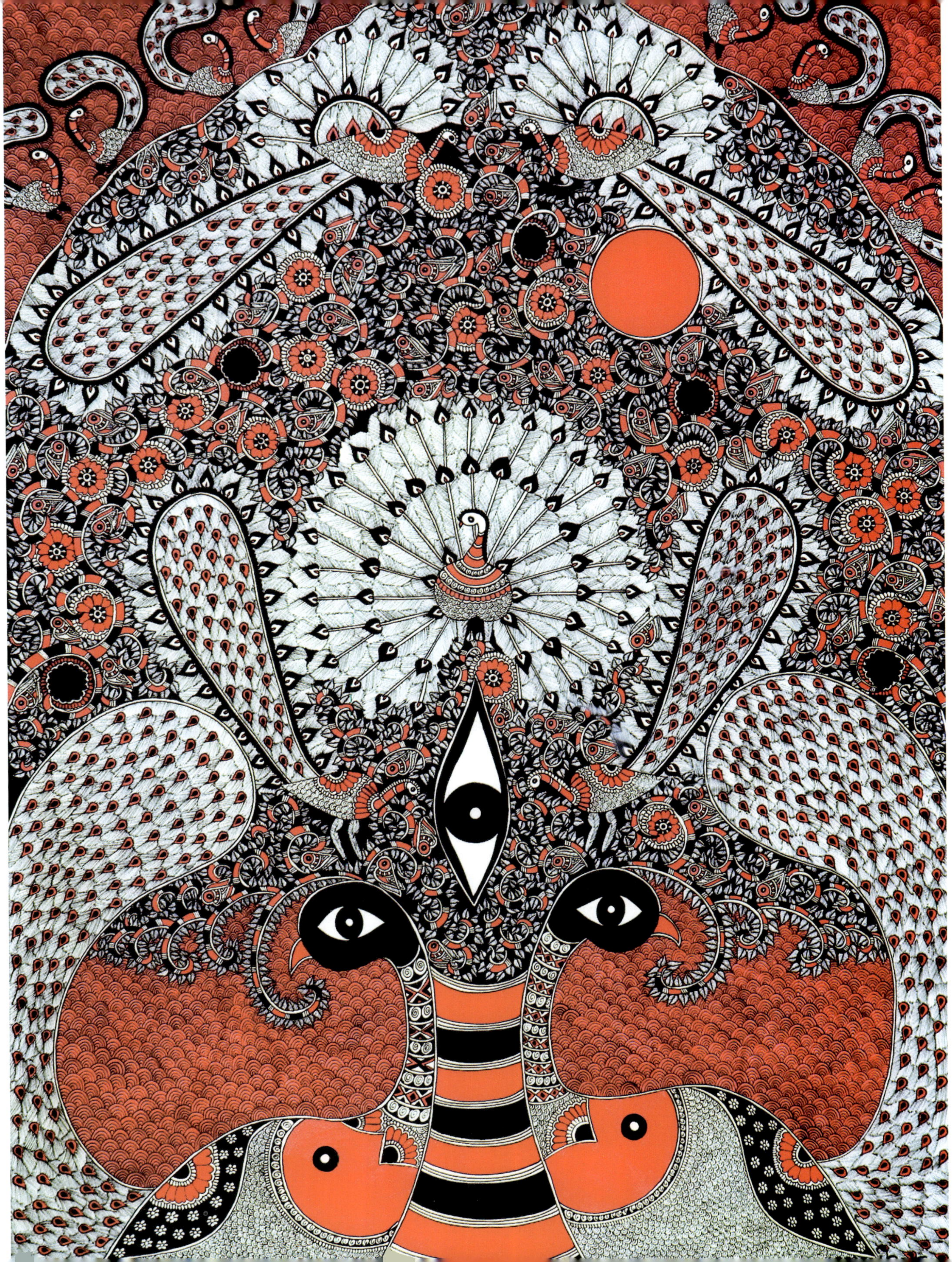

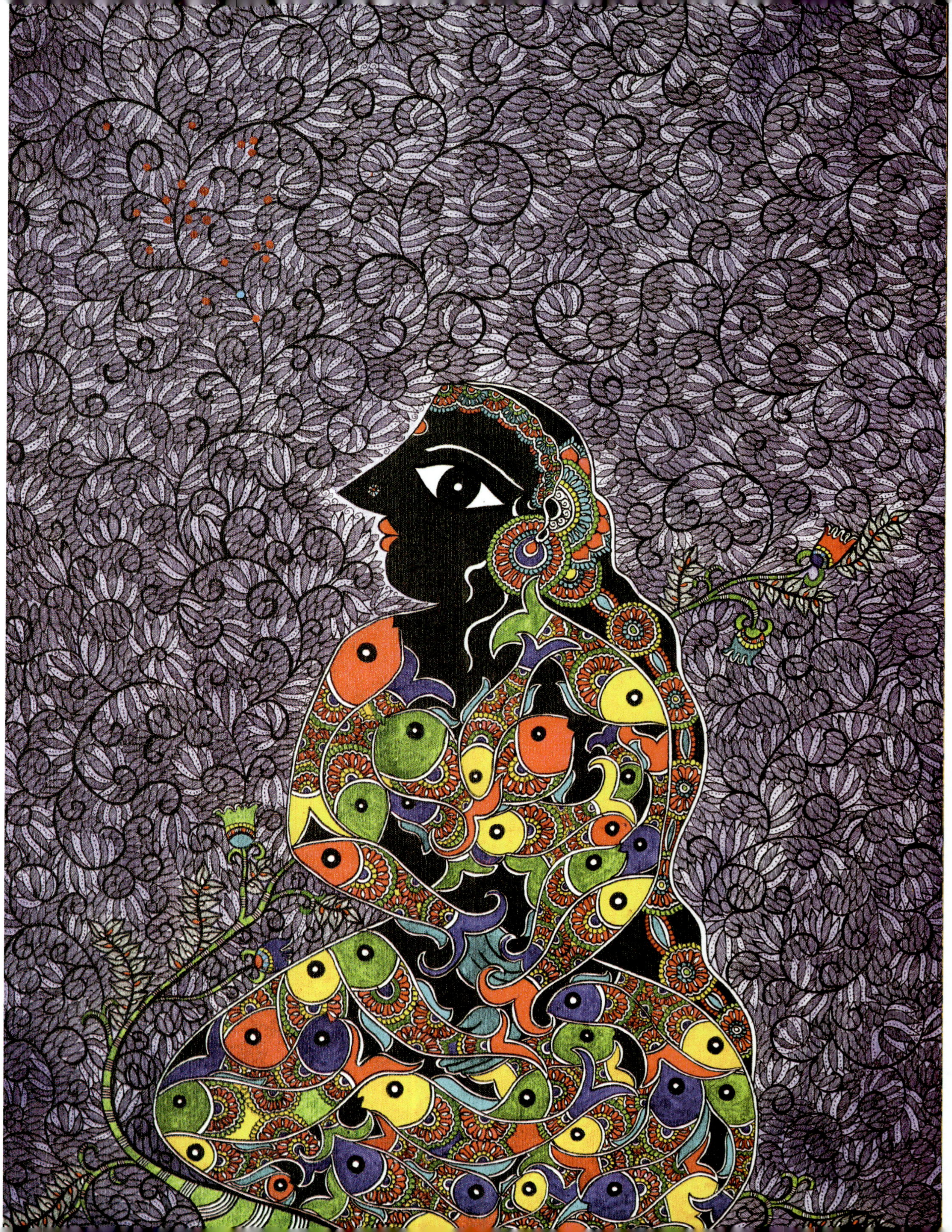

Dualism
Pigments on Paper, 73 x 52 cm (pp. 100-101)

The Tree of Life
Pigments on Paper, 99 x 70 cm (p. 102)

Peacocks
Pigments on Paper, 99 x 72 cm (p. 103)

Longing
Acrylic on Canvas, 93 x 70 cm (p. 104)

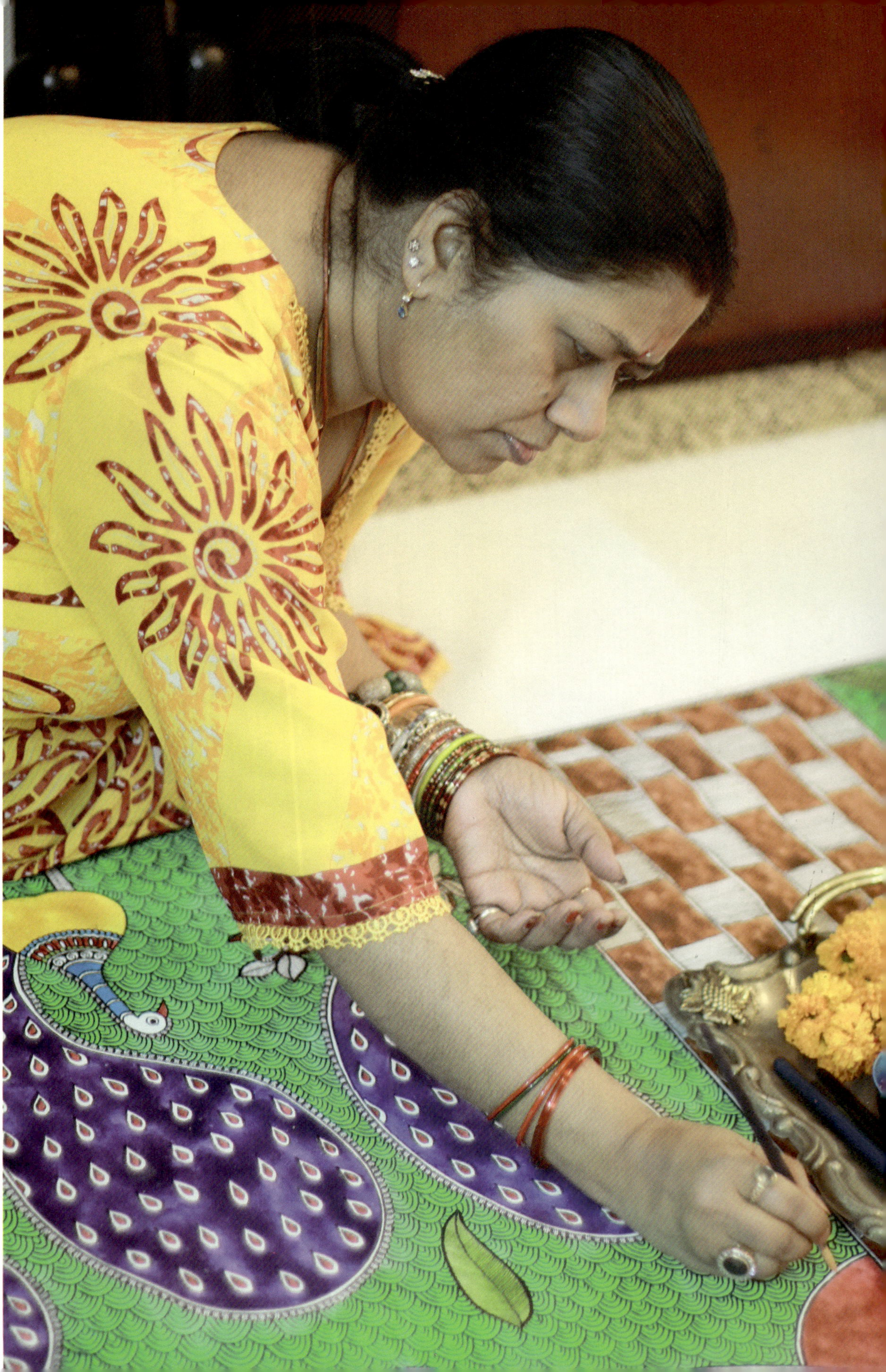

Bharti Dayal

Bharti Dayal, born 1961 at Samastipur, grew up in Darbhanga district of Bihar in Mithila region known for Madhubani folk style of painting. Though her formal education was in science and she holds a master's degree in the subject with a gold medal, she continued to learn painting from her mother and elders in the family, painting alpana on the floor and sketching epic scenes on the walls to celebrate auspicious occasions. Using natural vegetable dyes and crushed rice paste on handmade paper, cotton and silk fabric and canvases she continued to practice in her spare time to refine her skills. Marked for its rich colours and dense form, in Madhubani style, her art adorns a refreshing appearance given its assimilation of newer imagery with folk imprints and philosophical underpinnings. Showing professionally since 1991, her work has been exhibited in numerous shows across India and internationally. It can be seen at Bihar Pavilion, India International Trade Fair at New Delhi amongst others and in documentary films made by French Television and Discovery Channel. Winner of the State, AIFACS and Millennium Art Awards, she has also been helping promote work by women of her native village. Bharti lives in Delhi and works from her studio at home.

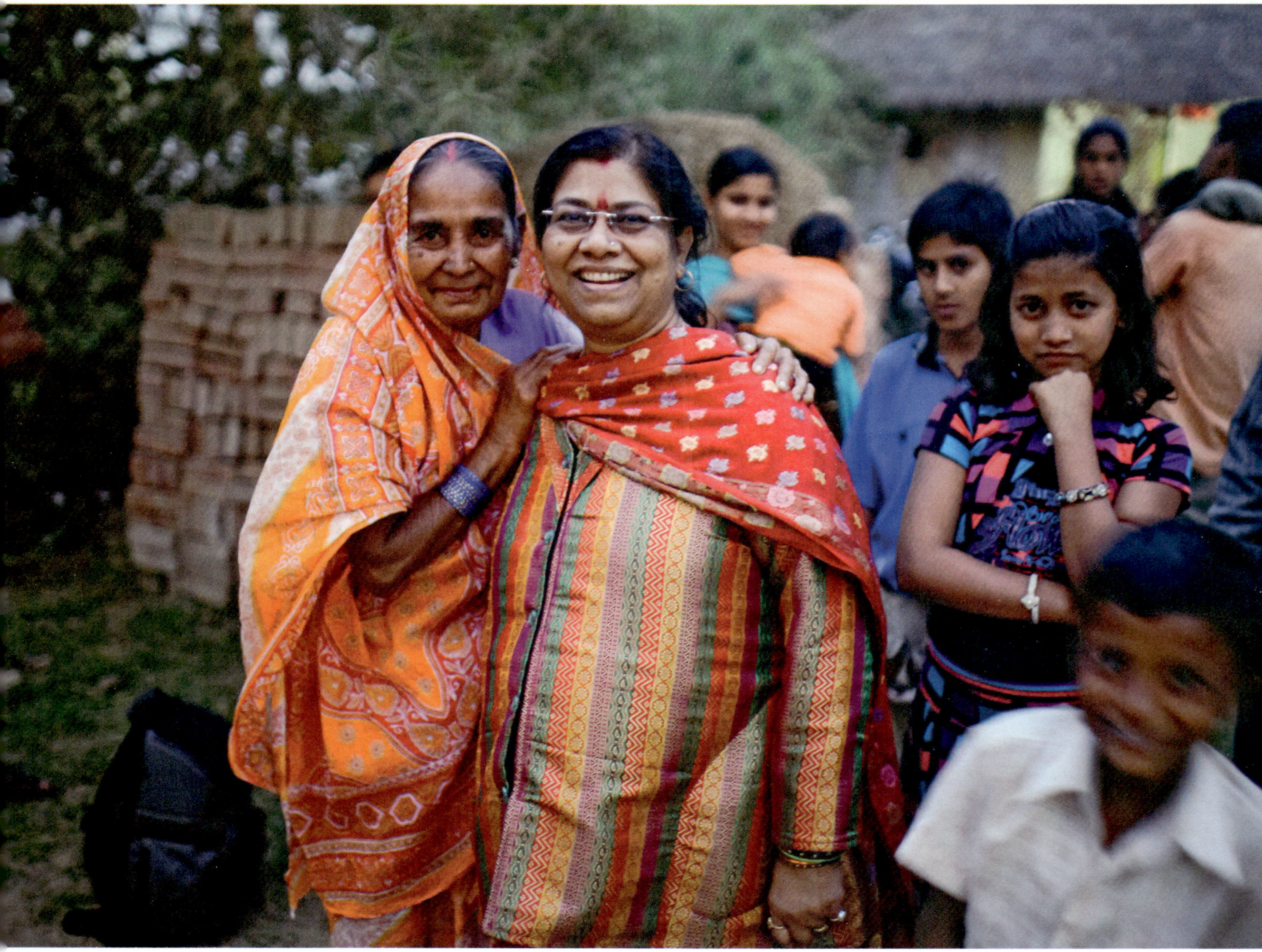